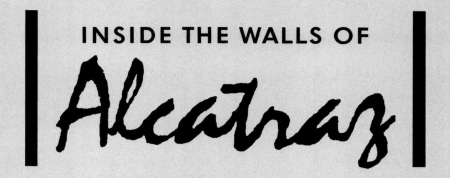

Frank Heaney

Gay Machado

Copyright 1987 Frank Heaney and Gay Machado
Copyright revised 1997

ISBN 0-915950-81-2

Printed in the United States
All Rights Reserved

Interior and cover design: Michelle Taverniti
Cover photo courtesy Golden Gate National Recreation Area

Library of Congress Cataloging-in-Publication Data:

Heaney, Frank, 1927-
    Inside the walls of Alcatraz.

    1. Heaney, Frank, 1927-   . 2. Correctional personnel—United States—Biography. 3. Prisoners—United States. 4. United States Penitentiary, Alcatraz Island, California. I. Machado, Gay. II. Title.
HV9468.H42A3   1987   365′.979461   87-876
ISBN 0-915950-81-2

Frontispiece: Cell bars in D-Block, Alcatraz Federal Penitentiary. *Courtesy Golden Gate National Recreation Area*

Acknowledgements

The authors wish to express their indebtedness to the following persons and organizations who gave their help and support in the production of this book:

Warden Swope who started it all.

Robert Kirby, former Alcatraz District Ranger who asked Frank to return to Alcatraz to serve as a Park Ranger.

Larry Quilligan, Frank's roommate on Alcatraz who contributed a number of materials to this book.

David Pence of the Red and White Fleet.

Terry Koenig of Catalina Cruises.

Brent Stienecker, Randy Collar and Ron Duckhorn of Crowley Maritime Corporation.

Park Historian James P. Delgado; District Ranger Colleen Collins; Park Rangers Richard Weideman and John Martini; and all the Alcatraz Park Rangers (Alcatroopers) past, present and future whose tales of Alcatraz make the island come alive.

The staff of the Golden Gate National Park Association.

The Alcatraz Alumni Association, a group of people that lived and worked on Alcatraz and for which Frank had the privilege of serving a term as President.

The staffs of the National Maritime Museum, San Francisco; Golden Gate National Recreation Area; the Bancroft Library of the University of California, Berkeley; the San Francisco Public Library; the *St. Louis Post-Dispatch;* the *Daily Ledger Post-Dispatch;* and the *San Francisco Chronicle* for their help in providing photographs for this book.

First and second overleafs: Aerial view of Alcatraz looking west, 1949. *Courtesy Pacific Aerial Surveys*

Third overleaf: Alcatraz prison inmates on their way to work in the prison industries, 1938. *Courtesy San Francisco Archives*

Fourth overleaf: Prisoners going through the metal detectors on their way from work, late 1940's. *Courtesy Golden Gate National Recreation Area*

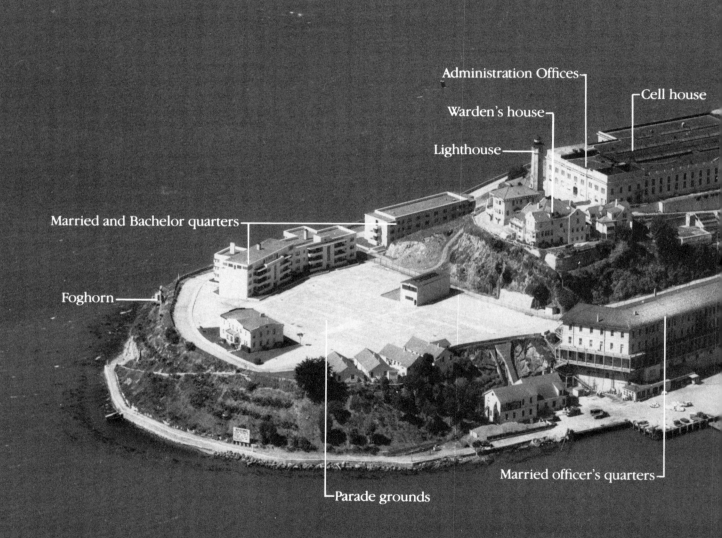

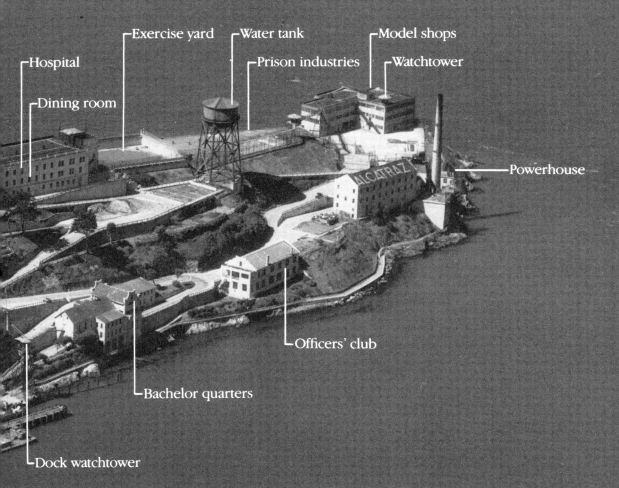

CONTENTS

From Pelicans to Penitentiary 17

I Was There; A Very Brief History; The Gangster Era; Open for Business

Frank 27

The Youngest Guard; Applying for the Job

Arrival/Physical Description of Alcatraz 33

What I Found—Entering Through the Security System; Hanging on to My Job; Intimidation; The Prison Itself; Dungeons; Solitary Confinement and Isolation

Life of a Prisoner 47

The New Prisoner; The Daily Routine; The Exercise Yard; Shaving; Reading, Movies, Religious Services; Violence; Holidays; Candy and Cigarettes; Meals; Billies, Handcuffs, and Blackjacks; Cellhouse Lawyers; The Real Terror of Alcatraz

Running Alcatraz 61

The Employees; A Guard's Life; Counts; Tier Duty; The Towers; Attention to Detail; Contraband, Drugs, and Sex; Dealing with the Crazies; The Bars; Disciplinary Measures; Running the Movies; Visitors; Sick Call; Nicknames

Notorious Prisoners   81

Machine Gun Kelly; Floyd Hamilton; Clarence Carnes;
Charles Berta; Creepy Karpis; The Nazis; Murder Incorporated;
Harmon Waley; Roy Gardner; Basil Banghart;
John Paul Chase; Cecil Wright; Al Capone;
Robert Stroud ("The Birdman of Alcatraz");
The Prisoner Mentality

Demonstrations and Escapes   99

Demonstrations; Early Escape Attempts; The Blast-out;
"Escape from Alcatraz"; The Last Escape

Afterword   123

The Death Penalty; Severity of Sentencing; Was Alcatraz
Necessary?

FROM PELICANS TO PENITENTIARY

I Was There

Alcatraz! Even now I feel a chill when I hear that name. Product of the gangsterism of the '30s, Alcatraz was the escape-proof prison that sealed men off from the normal world—a world from which the headliner criminals of the day disappeared, banished from all that made up the pleasures and satisfactions of life as we know them.

Inevitable rumors of inhuman treatment, and wasted, hopeless inmates kept the public fascinated with "the Rock." But for many years no reporters were allowed, visitors had no real access to prison life, and even Hollywood could only guess—and of course guessed the worst.

But I was there. I was the youngest guard ever to serve at Alcatraz, and I saw *first-hand* exactly what happened. I know that many of the horror stories had no basis in fact. But I also know that Alcatraz was indeed a living hell for many of its inmates—a hopeless, deadening end of the road. In a way I think it might have been worse than the stories the public *was* fed.

The story of Alcatraz, the Federal prison, is one of drab, lonely waiting, sudden bursts of violence and, yes, some harsh solitary confinement. It is also the story of some extraordinary people. But the best place to start is from the beginning...

A Very Brief History

The island was christened *La Isla de las Alcatraces*, island of pelicans, over 200 years ago, and that's what it was called when San Francisco Bay was a part of Mexico's California possessions. The first event of any interest was in 1846, when a man named Julian Workman petitioned the Mexican governor to establish a lighthouse on the island.

Before that lighthouse could be built, the discovery of gold at Sutter's Creek touched off a great migration of fortune hunters to California, which had just become part of the United States.

Opposite: A view of the island from the South. *Photo by Larry Molmud, courtesy* Daily Ledger Post-Dispatch, California.

Upper: View of Alcatraz and Angel Island from San Francisco, late 1800's. *Courtesy Golden Gate National Recreation Area.*

Lower: Original lighthouse on Alcatraz, commissioned 1854. Note cannon balls. *Courtesy The Bancroft Library.*

Commerce boomed in the Bay, much of it by sea, and the needed lighthouse was finally completed in 1854.

That's when the Army first took an interest in Alcatraz, and began construction of what was eventually known as Fort Alcatraz. Gradually the Army began to take advantage of the island's natural isolation and decided to house prisoners there. Over the years Civil War prisoners, Indians, Spanish-American War prisoners, and Army incorrigibles were all confined on Alcatraz.

Prison facilities were built, and proved adequate up until the turn of the century. But by 1903, the buildings were practically falling down, and plans were made for an essentially new prison facility.

Then the Great Earthquake hit. It was 1906, just before the construction work was to begin, but it really did no substantial damage on the island. In fact, the Army loaned its jails on Alcatraz to the city of San Francisco when the earthquake fires threatened the City's jails.

Between 1906 and 1911 the prison was essentially rebuilt, including the main cellhouse and support buildings that still stand today. But except for a spurt of usefulness during World War I, when it was used as an Army Disciplinary Barracks, Fort Alcatraz gradually fell into disuse.

In the late '20s and early '30s, the Army had its lowest enlistment rate in decades and, because of the lack of soldiers, there was naturally a lack of military prisoners. That's when the Army finally decided that Alcatraz was just too expensive to keep.

The Gangster Era

By coincidence, just at that time the Department of Justice was looking for something exactly *like* Alcatraz. Jailbreaks were epidemic. One fellow in particular, John Dillinger, had become expert at arranging escapes for his pals from Indiana State Prison. Finally he busted out of jail himself. Then Baby Face Nelson escaped, and Harvey Bailey, a companion of Machine Gun Kelly, broke out of Lansing. Escapees were killing guards, taking hostages, and terrorizing the countryside—even Leavenworth couldn't hold them.

The last straw was the "Kansas City Massacre." A group of criminals tried to break Frank Nash away from the FBI as they were escorting him to prison. They botched the job, killing several law enforcement officers and FBI agents, and Nash himself in the process. It was later suspected that it was a setup, that they actually planned to knock off Nash. Supposedly, Dillinger had something to do with it, and also Alvin "Creepy" Karpis, who I'll talk about later. I don't think the real truth was ever brought out.

Around this time, the Congress formed the Federal Bureau of Prisons. Until then, each Federal prison—and there were about four of them—was under its own jurisdiction, and each warden ran his prison more or less the way he thought it should be run.

Opposite, top: Army officers' family quarters, 1800's. *Courtesy Golden Gate National Recreation Area.*

Opposite, bottom: Garrison life on Alcatraz in the 1870's. Officers and their wives are in the garden in front of the army citadel. The cellhouse replaced this building in 1909. *Courtesy Golden Gate National Recreation Area.*

Above: Construction of the cellhouse, 1909. *Courtesy Golden Gate National Recreation Area.*

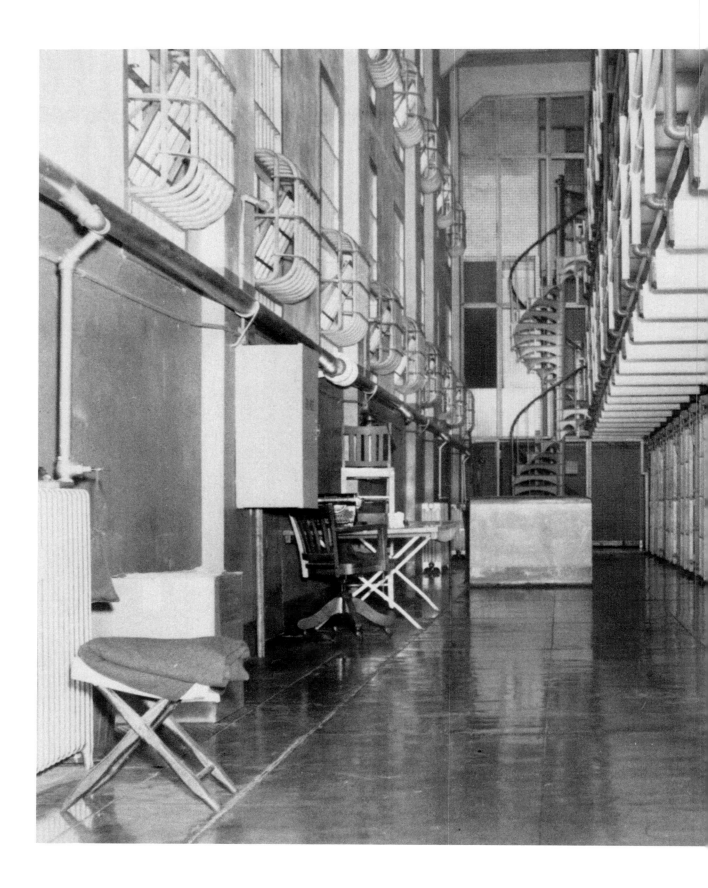

Left: The A-Block section of the Army prison. Note the flat steel bars. *Courtesy Golden Gate National Recreation Area.*

Above: B-Block. The ramp (later eliminated) led to the auditorium during the time it was an Army prison. *Courtesy* San Francisco Chronicle.

Eventually, things went crazy with favoritism and graft, until finally the Department of Justice made the decision to put one man in charge of the entire bureau. That first man was Sanford Bates. I remember his picture was in many of the books I got when I first started working on Alcatraz.

Alcatraz was built with one major thought in mind: to get those notorious criminals out of the limelight. They just loved the media attention—newspaper reports filled with their pictures, and radios announcing their names ten times a day.

It was thought that by putting these men away—locking them behind bars—keeping them away from the public where reporters couldn't ballyhoo their antics, crime would be reduced. And so Alcatraz was designed to be a place without privileges, with no trustees, no commissary, no organized sports, no honor system, and practically nothing to do. Originally, they even went so far as to include a strict rule of silence, while in line and during meals. (This proved unenforceable, however, and the idea was dropped.)

With very few exceptions, Alcatraz took no inmates directly from the courts; all were referred from other penitentiaries, and some state and military prisons if they had been a particular disciplinary problem. By the same token, inmates were hardly ever released directly from Alcatraz. Instead they were taken to other prisons to serve out the end of their terms. No one was ever paroled from Alcatraz!

Open for Business

In August, 1934, a group of fifty-three inmates was taken from Atlanta Federal Prison, chained hand and foot, and loaded onto a train headed for California. The train had special steel coaches with barred windows and wire mesh doors, because its cargo consisted of the most wanted criminals in the history of the United States penal system. One was Al Capone.

The train passed unannounced and unnoticed through the Southwest, while its passengers remained chained to their seats, unable even to use the bathroom except during specific times.

Because of the extraordinary security used for Capone, when they finally did reach the end of the line at Tiburon, California, the inmates were put directly on a railroad barge and shipped out to "the Rock." Even when they landed on the island, only their leg-irons were removed. Still handcuffed, they were marched up the hill and into the receiving station.

These big-shot criminals must have wondered what had happened to them. They were a beat-up bunch. They smelled, they were sweaty, and their feet were swollen from the chains.

You can bet they weren't ready to give anyone any trouble. After they were body searched, they were allowed to take a shower and then put on the standard prison uniform of denim shirts and pants. They were now official inmates of Alcatraz.

Train arriving with the first load of prisoners in 1934. *Courtesy Golden Gate National Recreation Area.*

FRANK

The Youngest Guard*

I was raised on Pat O'Brien and James Cagney movies—gangster stories—tales of robberies, kidnappings and killings. In fact, one of my earliest memories is of the Lindberg kidnapping. I was selling newspapers on the street corner at the time.

I used to go up to Shattuck Avenue in Berkeley, and I would walk down the block yelling, "Extra! Extra!" I must have been, oh, eight or nine years old. On almost every corner there was a kid hacking papers; we got a penny for each newspaper we sold, and I'd consider myself pretty lucky if I made ten cents in three hours' time. Ten cents in my pocket. That was pretty good money.

Every Saturday and Sunday, even in the poorest days, we'd go up to the United Artists Theatre—which is still located on Shattuck Avenue in Berkeley—for the matinees. I remember it cost ten cents to get in and my mother would give us each a penny for candy. On Saturdays, you could go into a five and dime, a Woolworth store, and get a "penny bag"—the broken-up candy that was at the bottom of the bin. You could get a lot of candy for a penny that way.

Gangster movies were real favorites with us kids. 'Course the story line was always the same: Pat O'Brien and James Cagney were growing up together in Hell's Kitchen, New York, and one of them would go bad. It was always Cagney. O'Brien would play the part of a priest, and Cagney a hoodlum. In the end, Cagney would repent, but, of course, he had to pay the price...sometimes with his life. I especially remember Pat O'Brien consoling Cagney as he was led to the execution chamber in "Angels with Dirty Faces."

That was the type of movie being made during the Depression. A lot of people sympathized with these movies' characters, and I think they must have had a great effect on me as well. Later in life, it made me more sympathetic to the lives of prisoners I had to oversee on Alcatraz, and we're talking about thieves,

Above: Frank receiving his First Communion, 1934.

Opposite: Frank Heaney, starting on "The Rock," 1948.

---

*With apologies to all my fellow correctional officers, I have frequently referred to us as "guards"—the title by which we are known to most of the public.

Upper: Frank age 15, 1411 Blake Street, Berkeley, California.

Lower: Frank in bootcamp, age 17, 1944, Brooklyn, New York.

murderers, rapists—the worst men society had to offer.

I was born and raised in Berkeley, California, during the Depression. My family was struggling like most were—nobody was too well off during those times. My dad worked two or three days a week is all. He was a bushelman—a tailor—a trade he learned in the Old Country.

Both my parents came from Northern Ireland. My mother was born in County Armagh and my father in County Down. They came to the United States from their predominantly Protestant areas because they realized their future was predetermined if they stayed. Dad came over about 1914, 1915, during World War I, and Mom in 1920. Funny thing is, they didn't know each other at all in Ireland. They met at one of the typical Irish community dances in San Francisco.

I remember my childhood years over-all as being very good, except for parochial school. I bridled under the strict educational system I was forced into at St. Joseph's Catholic School. I rebelled against the nuns every chance I got and, in return, I learned about corporal punishment. I was hit with rulers, locked in the closet, and whacked across the hand too many times to keep count. I was constantly after my mother to let me go somewhere—anywhere—and finally she relented, and I enrolled at Burbank Jr. High School in the seventh grade.

That was a change. I literally had to learn to do things all over again after doing my time in parochial school. Funny, that's exactly the way I thought of it...“doing time.”

Public schools were just the opposite: my first day in class I made the mistake of saying “Good Morning” to the teacher and I soon found out this was not the popular thing to do. I was quickly labeled a K.A., and had a few fights because of it.

In the latter part of junior and senior high, we all wore zoot suits, or “drapes” as they called them then. I can remember wearing a sports coat that went down to my knees and had slashed pockets and wide lapels. We had huge shirts with long collars and big wide ties, and our suspenders were always decorated with fancy stripes and bright colors.

My hair was quite long and swept into a ducktail. And when I was ready for a big night on the town, I'd slick it back and go to a dance hall in Oakland called Sweet's Ballroom at 14th and Franklin, a very popular spot. All the big bands played there: Stan Kenton, Woody Herman, Harry James, Jimmy and Tommy Dorsey, Jimmy Lunsford, Duke Ellington, Count Basie. Once, they even got Frank Sinatra.

I graduated from Berkeley High in 1944 at the age of seventeen and immediately joined the Coast Guard. I ended up in the Pacific Theater where I was assigned to a Coast Guard buoy tender. We followed the invasions, and we hit the Phillipines, Guam, Saipan, Eniwetok, and Guadalcanal.

There were some scary times, but I got through in one piece. When I got out in 1946, I enrolled in college in Berkeley. But I couldn't settle down to the school routine. I was primed for something to happen.

It was no help that I had been talked into being an accounting major. I never even liked math. When the opportunity to work on Alcatraz came along, I was definitely ready.

Applying for the Job

I had first learned about Alcatraz from my parents. We had taken many a trip on the ferryboat from Oakland to San Francisco (before the Bay Bridge had been built). On the way, my folks had told me stories about the men imprisoned there, and as a young teen-ager, I had been fascinated by that forbidding and lonely island.

In addition, I had always been fascinated by crime. I had taken an examination for the police department and was also thinking about working at San Quentin when the Alcatraz job came open. If it hadn't worked out, I was already on a list for the Alameda County Sheriff's Department.

My cousin Jimmy was a big influence in my decision, as well; he was a correctional officer at Folsom. I remember when I was about ten years old, he talked a lot to me about executions— hangings then, before they developed the gas chamber.

Jimmy said it was a pretty rough thing to watch, but they had to have witnesses at all the executions. Seems they would take the inmate into the execution area, which was really just a wooden platform with a trap door. They'd bring him in, put a cover over his head, and a noose over that. Someone would kill the ramp, and down the guy would go, his neck stretching until it snapped.

It was March of 1947 that I first saw the listing for an Alcatraz Correctional Officer, tacked up on a post office wall. I was ready. I'd ridden that ferryboat once too often—I thought I was going on an exciting adventure.

When I was being interviewed, the warden spent an hour and a half trying to convince me not to go to work on Alcatraz. That was Warden Swope, a very stoic kind of guy. He wore a big stetson and glasses, and he stared right at you like he wanted to make sure you knew who was boss. He might have smiled once in his lifetime; maybe not that much. But then, there weren't too many smiles on Alcatraz.

Warden Swope asked me why in the world I wanted this job. I told him my cousin had told me about it. He got into the fact of my being so young: "Young man, you are absolutely too young and immature for this job. We need older seasoned men. It will just be too difficult for you." And he didn't let up for a long time.

Eventually though, he relented. I guess I reached his conscience when I said that I had taken the examination in good faith, that I had scored quite high on the civil service test, and that I thought I at least deserved a chance. At any rate, he hired me.

Photo of Frank's trainee class (with backs to camera). The officials up front and facing the class are: Washington, Yocum, Madigan, Swope, Stucker, Eshelman, Kaeppel, and Rychner. *Courtesy Larry Quilligan.*

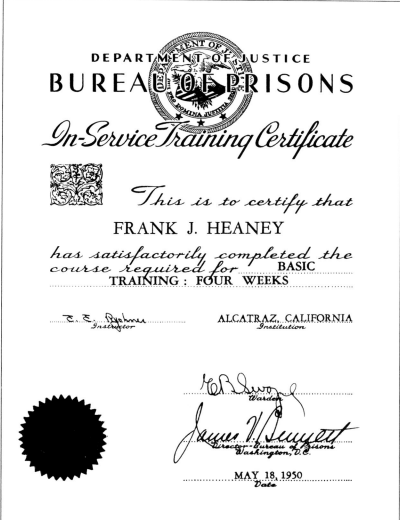

Certificate of completion of training.

ARRIVAL; PHYSICAL DESCRIPTION OF ALCATRAZ

What I Found—Entering Through the Security System

I still remember reporting for work the first day. As I entered the cellhouse, I had the same first glimpse that thousands of people had over the years—those who just came for a visit, and those who left great chunks of their lives there.

There was an officer outside in the sallyport area—the first holding area for anyone entering or leaving the cellhouse. I had to pass through three locked doors just to get into the inner section, and each door had a dual-control locking device. The officer on the outside had a key, and the officer in the control center had a lever. When the lever was pulled, the man on the inside could use his key to open the first gate. Once I was inside that area, the gate closed behind me and the lock was unreachable.

Then I went to the next set of doors, which had a shield plate over its lock; only when it was pulled back could the officer on the inside of that area unlock the gate. Finally, to get into the actual cellhouse, another officer opened a barred door and then a solid door. (No inmate was ever allowed near that area when the last two doors were being opened.)

Of course, all visitors who even landed at the dock had to go through a metal detector. One of the first stories I heard at Alcatraz was about Al Capone's mother and the metal detector. When she came to visit her son for the first time, she of course had to pass through the security system, and when she got to the metal detector, it went off. She went through again and it still kept buzzing. Finally, she was told the only way she would be allowed to enter was to have a security search, and so she was escorted to a dressing room by an officer's wife.

They found that the metal stays in her corset were setting off the alarm. It embarrassed her no end. When she reached the visiting area, she was plenty excited, and met her son with a volley of her native language, Italian. Of course, that wasn't allowed either. She was so upset by the embarrassment of the security check and her language problem, that she never returned to see her son on Alcatraz.

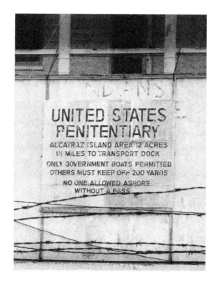

Below: Sign on bottom of family quarters that greeted visitors to Alcatraz. *Photo by Larry Molmud, courtesy* Daily Ledger Post-Dispatch, California.

Opposite: Alcatraz as seen from the Southwest. *Courtesy Golden Gate National Recreation Area.*

Above: Coast Guard quarters and lighthouse. *Courtesy Golden Gate National Recreation Area.*

Right: Looking south at recreation yard. Factory is in lower right-hand corner. A 250,000 gallon water tower is at center left. The hill guard tower is in the foreground. *Courtesy Golden Gate National Recreation Area.*

Hanging On to My Job

The first thing I did was to start looking for ways to show the warden that I was dedicated to my job, and also to develop a relationship with the prisoners in what I thought would be the right way. I went to the warden's office with a purchase slip for an idea I had—new phonograph records for the inmates. The warden did not take kindly to my suggestion—in fact he scared the living hell out of me.

He said, "Your job is to make sure the inmates are secure. Anything else is my job." With his cold steely eyes, and voice to match, he really dressed me down like I'd never had it before. I decided right then and there I wasn't going to do any favors for anybody. I'd just do my job and look out for myself.

But that wasn't the end of it. About a week after I was hired, Associate Warden Paul Madigan called me into his office. This was pretty common for new people, so at first I didn't think much about it. But though he tried to make me comfortable, it was soon clear that he wasn't happy about Warden Swope's decision to hire me.

Madigan never felt there should be guards as young as I. (Actually, in 1934, he had been one of the youngest correctional officers ever to work there himself.) They had a policy of only

Frank's efficiency rating notice.

picking the best men in the Bureau to work on Alcatraz—the ones who had worked with the worst prisoners in other Federal penitentiaries. Naturally, with my complete inexperience, they thought I would have a very difficult time. I reiterated that I should at least have the opportunity to try.

As he did with other officers during the one-year probationary period, Madigan would also, on occasion, call me in and evaluate me. My record was always "good." I never got an "excellent," just good. In their rating system I could have been fired. They didn't have to have charges. They could just have said I wasn't suited for the job.

Often they had difficulty placing me, because they didn't want me to have the responsibility of having too many inmates in my charge. I could understand that at first, but as time went on I was sure I could handle the situation. I felt I was very mature. I was getting tired of this song-and-dance about my youth and assumed immaturity, and I started to get angry; but I knew if I let it show, it would probably get me fired. So I set out to show Madigan I had the stuff to do the job, and do it well.

But it was a tough job steering clear of all the petty little regulations that came with my job. A short time after I started working in the cellhouse, one of them almost got me. One of the senior officers saw me with my hands in my pockets. This was a real no-no, and just the sort of thing that could get you fired. Since I was a new man, the officer wrote me up, and sent me back to the associate warden's office.

Madigan said, "Mr. Heaney, you were noticed with your hands in your pockets."

I said, "I guess I could have been; I'm not quite sure."

He asked if I had been warned about this, and I said "sure," but that I had seen other officers with their hands in their pockets at times and I didn't know it was all that important. I even was dumb enough to say, "In fact, I've noticed you with your hands in your pockets."

Well, he had a kind of reddish face, anyway, and it got even redder. "Boy!" he yelled at me, "Don't do as I do. Do as I say!" I must have been awful close to losing my job then. And I stayed close.

From then on, they never let up. When Madigan got tired, Swope would take over riding me. Madigan recommended that I would be better off at a clerk's desk, or some other type of non-custodial work. At one point, they tried to talk me into voluntarily transferring to work at the National School for Boys, a reformatory in Washington, D.C. I wouldn't even consider it. I enjoyed my work and I worked hard. But most of all I was beginning to get stubborn.

I felt that, if I left Alcatraz in that way, I would lose confidence in myself, I would lose my self-esteem (what there was of it), and I sure didn't want to become a failure. So I decided right then and there that if I did leave Alcatraz, I would do it under my own terms, and not because somebody else said I couldn't cut the mustard.

Intimidation

I had my first lesson in dealing with intimidation my first day on duty. I was walking down "Broadway," the main corridor between the triple-tiered cell blocks in the main cellhouse, and suddenly every inmate along the walkway started whistling and making obscene remarks.

I asked one of the older guards how to deal with it. He said there was only one way: "Ignore them. If you respond at all, they'll know they got to you and they'll never let up."

I wasn't really frightened, but I was so young and so new that at first the prison atmosphere did intimidate me. And I was bothered by the inmates' passive harrassment. I had been told inmates wouldn't attack you unless you stood between them and freedom, or if you agitated them excessively. But though the prisoners knew just how far they could go, I didn't.

Since an attack on an officer would land an inmate in solitary, harrassment was generally subtle. I remember once I had to bring a group of eight or nine inmates down to the shower room, which occasionally doubled as a band rehearsal room. I was standing by the stairs and they started rehearsing. All of a sudden they just quit. Then they turned in unison and stared at me. They just sat there silently, and I didn't know what the hell was going on. My imagination started to work, and I began to think about what to do if one of them started to come at me.

Then all of a sudden they started playing again. That was it. The whole thing took fifteen minutes or so, but I was dripping wet with perspiration by the time it was over. Later I learned that this was a common intimidation tactic, and one almost every guard had experienced. I just wish someone had told me ahead of time.

Dock tower. *Courtesy of Lt. Simpson.*

The Prison Itself

The main tower left today is the dock tower, and you can see it as you approach the island from the east side. We had other towers back in the '40s, all resembling each other: the road tower, which was on the west side of the island; the hill tower, which was in the middle and overlooked the industrial areas, the power house, and the northern part of the island; and there was the model shop tower (also still standing), which was manned during the day while the inmates were working down in that area.

We also had a roof tower, which was taken down while I was there. They didn't think they needed it—a big mistake. I believe it might have stopped the 1962 breakout. Although the inmates involved escaped in the dark of night, they had to do all of their preparatory work on the hatch that led to the roof, and would have been in clear sight of the roof tower.

One of the first things guests marveled at was the bulletproof glass armory. This was the control center for the entire island, manned twenty-four hours a day. There was a gatekeeper stationed at the front, but he wasn't allowed to unlock the doors until an armory officer looked through the glass panel and determined that everything was all right. Then the metal cover would be slid back and the door could be opened.

This was the real nerve center: we had telephones to the outside, loudspeakers, fire alarms, and a very sophisticated communication system, including the island-wide siren for emergencies. The various instrument switches were controlled from the single desk, within easy reach, and there was a rack that held keys for every door, shop, and gate on the island.

Many people expressed surprise at the quite decent condition of the cellhouses. They expected some kind of dungeon, I guess. We all tend to stereotype prisons, and one of the biggest surprises was that the cellhouses themselves were so well lighted. We had large skylights about four-and-a-half feet wide, which ran about 400 feet the length of the cell blocks.

Everything was quite meticulously clean: the galleries were always inspected; the rails were wiped down; windows were spotless; and the floors always dusted and polished. In fact, old army surplus blankets were used to polish the floors and bring up the sheen even more, till you could see your own reflection.

Dungeons

One myth about Alcatraz that was quite prevalent when I was there was that there were dungeons under the island, built by the Spanish. Actually, there were areas underneath, that originally had been used by the Army as a defensive barracks. It's also true that they had been used as cells, and it added to the myth that they were referred to as Spanish dungeons (though the Spanish never occupied Alcatraz).

What the Army did was to put bars in there and use them to keep the worst inmates (a practice continued after we took over in 1934). They were kept down there in complete darkness. At times they were chained up against the wall. (All this was described to me, and is not first-hand. But it was described to me by officers who did it—who were there.) Prisoners might be kept down there from a few days up to a week, depending on the same things as solitary in D-Block—the severity of the incident and the inmate's attitude.

The underground cells were used up until 1939-40, when a San Francisco judge declared that their use was unconstitutional, as cruel and unusual punishment. About that time they built the new isolation-cell wing in D-Block, and began using it for solitary confinement.

Photo page 41: A view of "Broadway" –the main aisle of the cellhouse. This was the least desired area because there was less privacy, it was colder than other cell blocks because the heat source was on the outside of the building, and there was less light since there were no windows. Black inmates were segregated in one section for most of the life of the prison. Broadway was also used to "quarantine" new inmates, and for the kitchen staff inmates. *Courtesy Golden Gate National Recreation Area.*

Above: View of officer in the control center. It was his responsibility to allow anyone in or out of the cellhouse. He was also in charge of firearms, and covered the phones. *Courtesy Golden Gate National Recreation Area.*

Right: Former army storage area converted to dungeons. Army inmates and Federal inmates were kept here for disciplinary reasons. The practice was stopped in 1939. The patched areas show where the bars were removed. *Courtesy Golden Gate National Recreation Area.*

Solitary Confinement and Isolation

There were two types of cells in D-Block: "Solitary" was a dark cell; "isolation" was a light cell. Solitary was nicknamed "the hole." There were 42 cells in D-Block. 5 were solitary cells with toilet and basin, 1 "strip cell," and 36 isolation cells.

The solitary confinement cells were similar to others on the inside, with a toilet and a basin, but on the outside there was a 200-lb. steel solid door, so that when you close it you're in complete darkness day and night. We'd issue a mattress in the nighttime—take it away during the daytime—coveralls and slippers.

The length of the sentence to solitary was determined first of all by the seriousness of the incident that got you there, and secondly by your attitude once inside those cells. They were like special attitude adjustment cells. Typical bad attitude would be shown by spitting on us, throwing food, urine or feces at us, cursing us. I've had all that thrown at me at one time or another. When you do that sort of thing, you stay in there longer. I heard it said that the official time was about 19 days, but they usually got out earlier, a few days to a week, if they behaved themselves.

We expected them to behave themselves, but these guys who got to solitary were pretty turned on, on a macho trip. A lot of them would be younger, and they would want to show the other guys on the outside that they were the real tough guys. It was a different world, a different society.

There was pride in being in there alone, pride in showing that they were tough—they could take it. And if they wanted to keep that up, then they'd be in there longer. Sometimes just a few days or a week, sometimes up to 19 days. Sometimes even longer, depending on how they acted.

If that didn't work there was the last cell—the strip cell. That one didn't have a toilet and a basin. All it had was a hole in the floor to go in. We called that a straight shot—"Oriental." They would sometimes be put in there without any clothing on— naked. We did that because they would be tearing up their clothing, and often their mattress and blankets. This would be taken as signifying that they did not want that clothing, or that blanket or mattress. So we would accomodate them and take everything away from them.

Generally speaking, time in that cell was very very short, maybe up to a maximum of a couple of days. Then we'd take them out and try them out again.

The inmates had an information pipeline that you can't believe. We tried to keep everything in isolation away from the general population inmates, but there always seemed to be inmates that would get information in and out. They knew almost everything that was going on—sometimes even more than we knew.

The isolation cells themselves were light, with regular bars. But those sentenced to isolation remained in their cells 24 hours a day. They were fed inside the cells. They only left for one hour a week by themselves out in the yard for recreation—and for a

15-minute shower at the other end of the block once a week.

How long they were inside these isolation cells would depend on the seriousness of the incident. The lower and second tier cells were used for those in for shorter terms. The upper tier, on the top, generally housed the longer term isolation inmates.

Robert Stroud was in cell 42 on the top tier. He remained in there until he left for the isolation wing of the hospital when he developed Bright's disease, a kidney condition. But he was in there for a long time. Also Whitey Franklin, an inmate who had been involved in a prison break years before, was in there for many years. Floyd Hamilton, the driver for Bonnie and Clyde, was in there for a number of years because he had been involved in a jail escape. Jail escapees generally stayed in there a long time. (Next to assaulting an officer, an escape was the ultimate crime.)

A view of the isolation cells in D-Block. The top right cell, #42, was home for Robert Stroud, "the Birdman," for a number of years.

Two views of the solitary confinement cells in D-Block. The left photo shows the thickness of the doors. The one on the right shows the observation window—which could be flipped open at any time by the guards to check on the inmates, then closed again, shutting out the light into the cell.

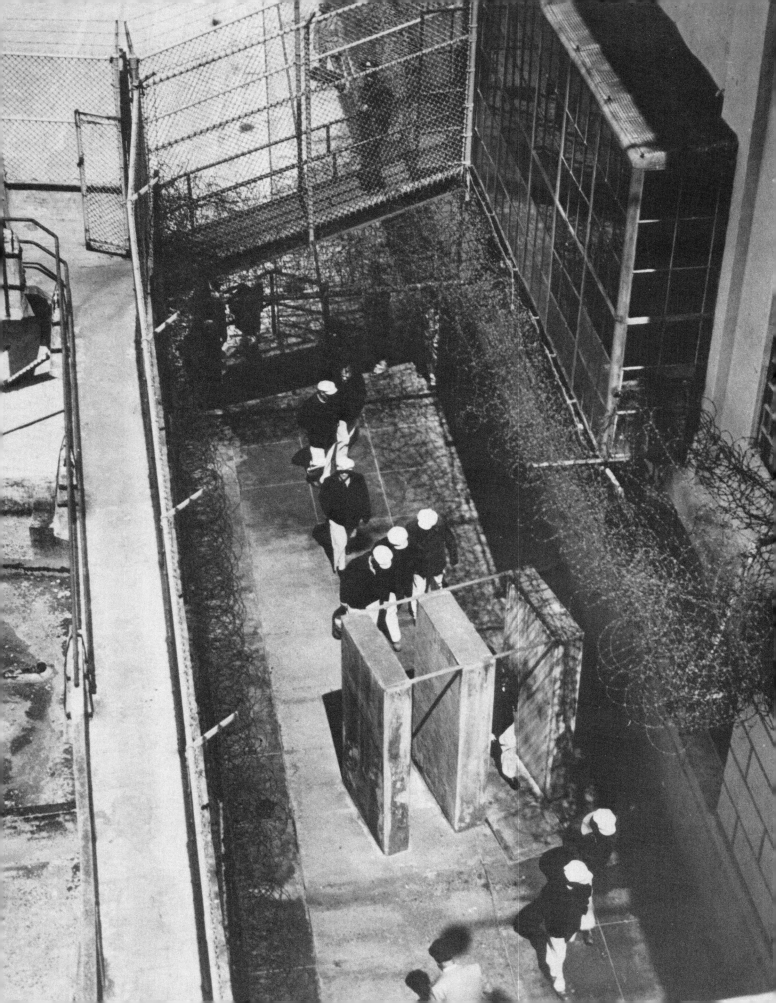

LIFE OF A PRISONER

The New Prisoner

When they first arrived on Alcatraz, inmates were stripped, searched and given a complete cavity exam. These were usually administered by the medical technicians, though sometimes we had to do it—it was not one of our favorite duties. They were also washed down in a dimly lit shower room. (From then on, they were allowed to return for a shower only twice a week.)

A new inmate was put into a quarantine unit on Broadway (the main cell block row), and kept there for up to a month. During that time he would be given shots, shown the rules and regulations, issued his clothing, and told about how to get by and be a good inmate.

He'd also be brought before a classification committee, made up of officials. (It could include the associate warden, the captain, a man from the industries, the chaplain, and perhaps a classification person from the office.) His background would be read, and he'd be asked what he'd like to do. They would describe the industries we had there, and try to learn what he might like to do and what he was qualified to do.

During that first month, if they wanted to work (work was a privilege), they might be allowed to sweep inside the cellhouse. Or they might be what they'd call a yardbird, down in the exercise yard, cleaning up after the people were out of there. He might do other types of somewhat menial work, eventually waiting for an opening in the industries. Other inmates could transfer around, and usually had priority, so it generally took some time before there was an opening.

One of the most desired jobs was to be an orderly in the library; they generally were long-term inmates.

The only jobs for which there was pay were down in the industries, and that started during the war. But there was the potential compensation of good time—a credit against length of sentence.

Opposite: Inmates walking through the metal detector, or "snitch box," from the recreation yard back into the cellhouse. *Courtesy Golden Gate National Recreation Area.*

Above: The uniform factory in the prison industries. *Courtesy Golden Gate National Recreation Area.*

Right: The prison laundry. With a contract carried over from the days of the Army prison, this was the largest military laundry on the West Coast; it used a tremendous amount of water. *Courtesy Golden Gate National Recreation Area.*

The Daily Routine

The daily schedule of the in-line inmates, inmates that were working during the week, would start when they were awakened at 6:30 in the morning. They would wash their faces (they didn't shave in the morning) and tidy up their cells. They had a little basket, that they would put whatever garbage they had in and leave outside the cells. And then they would stand for count.

After the count, they were taken to the kitchen for breakfast. They all marched in line, single-file, Block by Block. Generally they'd start on the outside upper tiers of B and C, and they'd march down, double-file into the eating area. They had about twenty minutes to eat their meal.

When they finished their breakfast they'd be marched down into the yard, where there were stripes marked to line them up according to where they worked. Lined up there, we'd count them again, and then they'd file down to where they worked—down to the stairs between the yard and the industrial area, and into the industries. As soon as they were all inside the industries, another count, and then work.

They'd leave the work areas about 11:30 to be marched back up to the cell house again. They would change into coveralls and go into the dining hall, eat, come back out to their cells, and stay in there for about twenty minutes unless they went on sick call. If somebody was sick he'd go up to the hospital and see the MTA (medical technician), and if necessary the doctor.

And then they'd go through the same procedure again—down into the yard and the industries. They'd work until about 4:30, when they would be brought back into the cells again. They'd be brought into the dining room, fed, and be back at about 5:30 inside their cells. (Of course there would be repeated counts throughout the process.)

That was the end of the day. The day shift was usually dismissed once the prisoners were locked up. At 9:30 we turned off the lights.

The Exercise Yard

The exercise yard was used during the week by isolation inmates individually, or sometimes two or three at a time if there were too many for the allotted time. It was also used during the week by the inmates who worked in the kitchen, because they worked seven days a week. And some inmates who had special privileges were allowed out during the week for an hour or so. So there was always one of us up above, walking around with a gun, and at least one or two officers down in the yard watching the inmates.

Out in the yard, inmates were allowed to play bridge, checkers, dominoes, and chess. And they devised their own game called "Name That Ship." One inmate would sit at the very top of the

Below, left: Inmates in the recreation yard, here playing cards while guards observed. The only "card" game allowed was bridge, using dominos rather than cards. Cards would wear out too fast, would blow away, and the cellulose coating could be scraped off to make an explosive. *Courtesy Golden Gate National Recreation Area.*

Below, right: The south end of the recreation yard, with inmates playing handball against the prison wall. The "road" guard tower is on the right. *Courtesy Golden Gate National Recreation Area.*

stairs and watch the Golden Gate Bridge. As a ship came through, he'd try to describe it: tonnage, type of vessel, and other things he'd memorized from a Navy book, *Jane's Fighting Ships,* we had in the prison library. The other guys down below would try to guess the name of the ship.

The most popular sport in the yard was handball—played against the wall. They had to buy all the supplies themselves. They were allowed to buy the balls and handball gloves.

Softball was played usually on weekends. The only difference between softball at Alcatraz and softball outside was that if you knocked the ball over the wall you're out. (It was not a home run, and you couldn't go out and get it, either.) We usually had an inmate that worked outside the wall—the gardener. He would throw them back.

Shaving

Shaving was strictly enforced. When I worked the 4:00 p.m. to midnight shift, one of my responsibilities was to issue a razor blade to each inmate. He could keep it inside his cell for thirty minutes only. I had a small board with a hook on the end and, sometime around 6:30 p.m, I'd go to each inmate and put his blade on the lip of the cell. Exactly one half-hour later, they'd better have that blade back in place. Otherwise, it was solitary confinement.

We supplied all inmates with cheap little double-edged razor blades and a sharpening device, a small piece of leather. They each had a shaving mug, but some just preferred to use soap and water.

If an inmate refused to shave—and on occasion one would—three or four officers would be called in to hold him down for a dry shave, as an example for the other inmates. If you've ever had a dry shave with a cheap government-issue blade, you know why we didn't have that problem too often.

I never saw anyone attempt to commit suicide with a blade, but I heard several tried. My personal belief is that they wanted more to attract attention than anything else. However, if a prisoner drew enough blood and made it look bad enough, he could get sent to Springfield Hospital in Missouri, a prison hospital for medically and mentally ill inmates. That was a definite step up from Alcatraz.

Reading, Movies, Religious Services

The prisoners had no television, radio, or newspapers, and only a limited number of magazines; but they did have a library of about 15,000 books left over from the time Alcatraz was an army prison. It was pretty extensive—mostly light reading materials—but some good novels. I remember Zane Grey was quite popular, and also Jack London. Of course, they could have nothing that contained any sex, violence, or crime—which was a difficulty then, an impossibility today.

The inmates would have in their cells a catalog of the books. They could fill out chits, drop them in a box on the way to the mess hall, and the orderlies who worked in the library would run carts along and bring the books to the cells later that day.

The library also had information about books that were available so that inmates could order books. In addition, inmates could subscribe directly to approved magazines. The most popular were *Life, Time,* and *Newsweek.* Any of the unapproved material would be cut out. When any inmate who had subscribed directly for it was finished with a magazine, he could forward it to a friend, and it could go on to subsequent prisoners in that fashion.

If an inmate couldn't read, he was in a whole lot of trouble because that was the main occupation between 5:30 and 9:30 p.m. when the lights went out. That's when they would start flipping out—when they had nothing to occupy their minds.

"One Day at a Time"

Robert Stroud, "The Birdman of Alcatraz," used to say to the other inmates, "You just got to take it one day at a time." Another inmate, John Chase, was more specific: he'd say you have to live from one experience to the next—no matter how trivial. Just look for one little pleasure. Take breakfast, for instance; you could look forward to having pancakes. It was very important to them to have a decent meal.

One of the Catholic chaplains who served during the late 40's and early 50's. *Photo by Lt. Simpson.*

Or you could look up at the sky and watch the clouds go by. You could stare at the Golden Gate Bridge, count ships, whatever. You could dream, or wait for a library book you wanted to read, or wonder who's gonna win the next softball game. That's really all they had left.

I remember showing movies on Alcatraz about once a month, usually on holidays. As with everything, movies were a privilege. You had to be a "main line" inmate—a good inmate—obeying the rules and regulations, and your movie privileges were just another thing that could be taken away at a disciplinary hearing.

As with the books, movies on Alcatraz could not show any crime, violence, or sex. Shirley Temple was one of the cons' favorite actresses. Mine too.

We had Catholic services one week, Protestant the next, and, for awhile, we had a Protestant chaplain living on the island full time. Families never attended mass with the inmates; officers (including me) would only observe. The one person I recall attending mass with the prisoners was Associate Warden Paul Madigan, and Warden Swope later put a stop to that.

Violence

After seven days a week pent up in five-by-nine-foot cells, frustration was high and violence common. Over long periods of time these men would build up animosity towards each other, animosity that sooner or later was often gratified. The means was usually by knifing. Generally they would not have a conventional knife, but something that was probably manufactured from a kitchen utensil, perhaps a fork or a spoon. It might be a wooden instrument—anything that was sharpened.

The assailant would generally get about four, five or six of his buddies involved, always down in the yard. Those involved would quickly surround the one that was going to get stuck. The man with the grudge would move in and stick the victim, sometimes in the side, sometimes in the stomach—generally not in a vital area—trying to hurt him but not kill him. Then they'd quickly walk away. If they killed him, the FBI was always brought in. And the FBI was relentless in finding out who did it. We caught quite a few—but if we didn't get the guy, well . . .

I know that when I worked in the yard and I saw a quick surrounding of an inmate, I knew that something like that would be happening. I'd go over there, but by the time I'd got there the guy would already be stuck, and usually the weapon would be lying on the ground, because they didn't want it anymore. There would be no fingerprints on it—they'd make sure of that.

And when I or another officer got there, we'd ask the inmate what happened. You always asked that but you knew that you always got the same response: The inmate did not know what happened; he didn't know who did it; he didn't see it. And the inmates around there would not have seen the incident.

No inmate ever saw such incidents, because that's the number one rule among inmates—you never tell The Man what's happening. So sometimes they were caught and sometimes, maybe 50% of the time they weren't.

When we thought we had the assailant, he would be brought before the trial board. (This was the tribunal used for the most serious offenses.) The trial board was made up of the associate warden, sometimes the captain, the chaplain, a lieutenant, and occasionally (not often) one of us. All the known facts of the case were brought before them, but since the inmates would never testify, we seldom had much proof.

Often there would be no punishment, though it would really depend on the trial board—who was on it and how they wanted to do it. If they really wanted to stick a guy, and it was someone who was having a lot of problems, they were free to treat the case as they saw fit. This wasn't a trial in the way that you go to court, and there wasn't any appeal. You didn't have to answer to anybody.

Holidays

I happened to be working on Alcatraz the first time they put up a Christmas tree, in 1948. I helped decorate it; we wouldn't let the inmates do it. It was in the dining hall where everyone could see it and walk by it. I have no idea whether it brought more joy or sadness.

New Year's Eve was one time the administration let the inmates let off a little steam. They would holler, howl, and take tin cups and run them up and down the bars. It was the one time they were allowed to express their feelings about things they didn't like.

Occasionally things got a bit out of hand. They would throw toilet paper all over the block and try to light their cells on fire. If they succeeded, we would hose down the cell with the inmate inside. There were a lot of stories about the hosing going on all the time, but, to my knowledge, this was the only time and the only cause.

Candy and Cigarettes

Alcatraz had no commissary like other penitentiaries. The inmates had no tailor-made cigarettes, no candy bars, no chewing gum, and no soft drinks. So the bit of candy they got at Christmas time was a really rare treat. The associate warden would go around with a little holiday box of hard candy, and maybe a half-dozen packs of cigarettes—cheap Wings cigarettes.

To prevent bargaining and gambling, prisoners had only two-to-three weeks to consume the Christmastime gifts of food, candy, or cigarettes. Anything found in a cell after that time was considered contraband and the inmate was subject to disciplinary action. He usually lost yard privileges, or maybe his job was taken away; once in awhile he got the extreme sentence of going to solitary confinement or isolation.

The prisoners had accounts out of which they could buy such things as painting supplies, musical instruments, approved books and magazines. They could not buy candy or rolled cigarettes. The cigarettes that were available were roll-your-own. They could keep one open and one unopened pack inside their cell.

Quite often, inmates would try subtle ways to get me to bring in candy or cookies or sweets. For example, one would say to me, kind of pleading like, "Gee, Mr. Heaney, what does a Mr. Goodbar taste like nowadays? Do they still have nuts in 'em like they used to?"

One guy had a craving for fig bars; he always wanted to talk about fig bars. He'd tell me over and over how he loved them as a kid. After a while—even though it drove me crazy—I began to really sympathize with him, because when I had been overseas in the military, I'd had the same kinds of cravings myself.

But I was afraid that if I ever gave in to their requests, I would be compromised. I didn't want them to have something on me, and of course I didn't want to be caught by the administration either. But the inmates always kept trying, and I did feel sorry for them.

I've been told that some officers did bring in a few things for their favorite inmates: candy bars, chewing gum, cigarettes. Eventually, I was tempted to do the same thing because, I have to admit, there were inmates I started to take a real liking to. But I was too scared to break the rules. In a sense, though, I began to admire some of the convicts, or perhaps just their courageous defiance.

Meals

Meals on Alcatraz weren't too bad. They were just repetitious, like military food. And that was because we were on such a low budget. Once the steward told me he was supplying food for the current inmate population on the same budget he had had years before.

Inmates were never allowed to bring anything out of the dining room. Every piece of food on their trays had to be consumed; if not, and if an inmate were caught, he would be subject to strict disciplinary action.

Sometimes we had a problem with the inmates who worked in the kitchen putting soap in the food. Guards had to taste everything before it was served, which always made me a little nervous. And, if we had to dispose of the food, the inmates would start hollering, and we'd end up serving them sandwiches in their cells.

Officer standing in the inmates' dining hall. No knives were allowed, only forks and spoons. *Courtesy Golden Gate National Recreation Area.*

Billies, Handcuffs, and Blackjacks

Gas billies were clubs with a teargas device that could be triggered off. In the early years I understand they were carried by some of the officers, but by the time I got there they had stopped, because they found out they were very cumbersome, and they also came to realize that if the billies were used, everybody would get gassed. I never saw one exploded. They were accessible though, and theoretically could have been used.

We did use what we called a come-along, which is a kind of handcuff. When you put it on an inmate and squeezed it, the handcuff got very tight. Once an inmate realized that the more he struggled the more it would hurt, he usually quieted down. As I remember, it was not an official device. But some officers used it on their own.

Inmates entering dining room from the cellhouse. They all filed in in the order of their cells (no random seating was allowed), stood until their table was filled, and then sat down in unison. *Courtesy Golden Gate National Recreation Area.*

Some of the more senior officers carried blackjacks. A blackjack is a short club made of lead, covered with leather. We were not allowed to carry regular clubs, but sometimes there was a real need.

You go up against an inmate—and some of these guys were a lot stronger than you—and you've got to have an equalizer, something to get a guy down; otherwise you're going to get hurt. I've been hurt and you get tired of getting hurt. You've got to use something to remedy a situation fast. A blackjack was about as good as any.

It was illegal to carry them, and you could have been brought up on charges if you were carrying a blackjack. But a number of the senior officers carried them. I never witnessed an officer using a blackjack unless it was really needed—in self defense, taking a nut out of his cell, something of that order. I can't talk for all the times, but I never saw an improper use of a blackjack.

Cellhouse Lawyers

Cellhouse Lawyers were prisoners who spent all of their time reading law books, and representing themselves and other inmates in their appeals. The most popular subject for library requests was law—criminal law dealing with the procedures for getting yourself out of prison.

The first thing they would do—the cellhouse lawyers—would be to get the trial transcript, and then pick it apart looking for any mistakes that had been made that could provide the basis for a writ of habeus corpus. Apparently during the '30s it wasn't uncommon for a prisoner to act as his own counsel in serious cases. In later years, courts ruled that self-representation in effect deprived them of a fair trial—that, without the assistance of a trained lawyer, the accused could not be assumed to properly understand the nature of the charge or the legal proceedings. This became the basis for many of the appeals of inmates who had represented themselves in their trials.

Prisoners with the skill and knowledge to write good appeal petitions were being granted new trials. Some of the prisoners had become more expert at criminal appeals than their lawyers. I have been told frequently that some of the Alcatraz prisoners showed legal artistry comparable to that of the most experienced members of the bar.

Many of the prisoners' protests sought relief other than their release: Sometimes they protested prison regulations; sometimes they wanted to regain time credits that had been forfeited; they at times charged brutality on the part of the prison officers; and sometimes they questioned the right of the Federal Government to transfer a man to Alcatraz at all.

In the last instance they would claim that serving time on Alcatraz stigmatized them—that they became more vicious, hardened, and impossibly incorrigible after a few years on "Devil's Island." They said no one should be kept in a place like Alcatraz.

The Real Terror of Alcatraz

I personally think what got to them was the length of their terms and the utter boredom of life in that most extreme of prisons. With all the sensationalized rumours of brutality and inhuman confinement, critics missed the main point: The terror for those who could not take it came not from physical abuse, but from boredom.

One of the most precious privileges—ironically for men who had flaunted normal social values—was to have a job. But even with one of the better jobs, in one of the prison industries, they still worked with the same people every day, in the same place, doing the same thing.

Eventually, many of the prisoners I knew would decide to just hole up in their cells and become totally reclusive. They'd tell me they couldn't stand to hear the same stories day after day—year after year in some cases. You can imagine: day after day, night after night in the same cells, with absolutely no variation, and nothing to look forward to.

Inside one of the isolation cells in D-Block. *Courtesy Golden Gate National Recreation Area.*

RUNNING ALCATRAZ

The Employees

The day-by-day security of the prison was of course the responsibility of the correctional officers. The over-all responsibility was held by the wardens. In total, Alcatraz had four wardens: Warden Johnston, who left about the time I was hired, was the first; Warden Swope, the man who actually gave me the job was second; then Warden Madigan; and then Warden Blackwell, whom I did not know.

Warden Johnston was a short, stodgy, grey-haired gentleman; I have fond memories of him. He had been a warden at Folsom many years before and had succeeded in straightening it up. When he left, it was a very well-run prison. Later, he was the warden at San Quentin. In 1934, he had left the penal system and was, in fact, in banking when he was called and asked to be the first warden on Alcatraz.

Not long ago, I met his daughter, Barbara Johnston, at a 50th anniversary reunion on the island. She is a very gracious woman and told me she had many good memories of living on Alcatraz. Though he ran a tough, no-nonsense program, Warden Johnston was very well liked.

Warden Swope, on the other hand, got mixed reactions from most of the personnel and inmates. He was somewhat of a hardliner and many rebelled against that. I remember Robert Stroud hated him. Johnston had allowed Stroud to do research on his birds; he didn't have any actual birds in his cell, just plenty of correspondence and textbooks and such. But Swope started taking those privileges away, limiting his writing materials and the amount of time he could spend in research. I guess he felt Stroud shouldn't have any more privileges than any other inmates.

There were other employees who worked, and sometimes lived on the island. There was a member of the coast guard who answered to the warden, and lived there with his family. In the earlier days before automation (in the '50s), there had been a full-time lighthouse keeper who also lived on the island with his family.

There was also the staff of the Public Health Service. The

Opposite: Guards warning small boats carrying members of the press to stay away from Alcatraz Island during the 1946 blastout. *Courtesy National Maritime Museum, San Francisco.*

Below, left: Warden James A. Johnston, who served 1934-1948. *Courtesy Golden Gate National Recreation Area.*

Upper, right: Warden Edwin Swope, who served 1948-1955. *Courtesy Golden Gate National Recreation Area.*

Lower, right: Warden Paul J. Madigan, who served 1955-1961. *Courtesy Golden Gate National Recreation Area.*

Above: The warden's home. Prior to this it was the home of the Army commandant. It had 18 rooms, two stories and a basement, two fireplaces, and a panoramic view of San Francisco. *Courtesy Golden Gate National Recreation Area.*

Left: The doctor's home on Alcatraz. *Courtesy Golden Gate National Recreation Area.*

doctor when I was there was a full commander in the Public Health Service, named Richard Yocom. He lived right next to the Warden's house. They also had the medical technician attendants—some of whom lived on the island. Then they had the civilian workers who worked in the industries as foremen. Finally, there were the administrative personnel.

About 50% of the staff lived on the island and 50% commuted. Generally there were not enough living facilities for those that wanted them. Most of the men who came to Alcatraz had been transferred there from other parts of the country, and arrived without a place to live. San Francisco was relatively expensive, even then, and it was both cheaper and more convenient to live on Alcatraz Island, and not to commute. Sometimes they didn't have to have a car. So there were people who wanted to live on Alcatraz.

A Guard's Life

Personally, I didn't mind the living conditions at all. I lived in the bachelor quarters of the converted military chapel. For $10 a month, I got a bed and bureau, and my laundry done. Either I ate the same food as the inmates, or I ate with one of the families on the island, or I went into San Francisco for meals.

There was a lot of recreation for us: bowling and billiards, dancing and card playing. There was a handball court that doubled as a gymnasium, a kid's playground, and places for picnicking, fishing, and crabbing. Female guests of single men were not allowed in our quarters; but our male friends and relatives could be entertained anywhere in the residential areas. And it was a big deal to be able to invite someone to visit you on Alcatraz. I never knew I had so many friends.

All women and children on the island were required to avoid contact with the prisoners, a rule not too difficult to enforce. On the other hand, with special permission from the warden, my male friends could be taken on an escorted tour of the prison.

But even with the pleasant facilities, at my age going to work on Alcatraz was like being an inmate, even when I had time off and was in my bunk area. Two or three times a week I'd have to get on the "Warden Johnson," the diesel-powered prison launch prisoners had built, and go into San Francisco. That was the only way I could get my head together and get away from the atmosphere of the "Big House."

As a rule, the officers on the island hadn't applied there because they thought they would like it, but rather to get a promotion. It seemed that to get ahead in the Federal penal system you had to do a little time on Alcatraz, so to speak. But after they had lived there a while, they often got pressure from their families to remain.

People got used to living so near San Francisco—right in the middle of things. Many of these families had been transferred

Upper: The former military chapel, used as bachelor quarters (where Frank lived) during the Federal penitentiary period. *Courtesy Golden Gate National Recreation Area.*

Lower: Former military parade ground, which became the recreation area for the families of prison personnel. Note the handball court and children's play area in the foreground. *Courtesy Golden Gate National Recreation Area.*

Upper: The prison control center, where the officers called in their prisoner head-counts. All telephone and radio communication with the mainland was centered here. *Courtesy Golden Gate National Recreation Area.*

Lower: All prison keys were kept in the control center. *Courtesy Golden Gate National Recreation Area.*

from prisons located out in the boondocks and this was a pretty exciting place for them. So I knew a lot of officers who would have been just as happy to leave the island, but never felt they could. In one way or another I guess we all felt trapped.

The Government Store carried a full line of supplies, and was open a few hours in the mornings and afternoons. It was located next to the post office (also run by officers' wives), and all outgoing mail was stamped with an Alcatraz postmark. Though the inmates weren't too fond of the postmark my friends certainly were. They would ask me to bring their mail back to the island and mail it from there just so it would have the Alcatraz postmark.

Counts

On Alcatraz we had about twelve official counts a day, accounting for all of the prisoners. The guards were required to call and report in to the control center, which was the area in front of the cellhouse in the administration wing. While the control center officer tallied the results of the counts, inmates were not allowed to move. Absolutely nothing was done until the official count was okayed.

But you were also expected to do your own checks, about one every fifteen minutes; so you were *constantly* counting the prisoners. Obviously, it would have been very difficult for an inmate, especially during the day, to take off and make his way down to the water.

Tier Duty

Each tier had an officer. There were three tiers in each of the two main cell blocks—B and C—so there were six officers assigned there.

One of the first things I was taught on tier duty was never to follow a routine: You avoided getting into a set routine for patrolling the cell fronts; you altered the directions you walked along the galleries; if you worked in a gun gallery, you didn't even go to the toilet at the same time every day. The inmates were always looking for one little way, one more weakness in the system that they could take advantage of, where they could find an opportunity to try and escape.

Inmates were required to stand in front of their cells while we walked down the tiers and counted them. They were required to stand at attention; the only time they didn't have to was if they had to urinate or have a bowel movement. Then they could sit on or stand in front of the toilet.

Coincidentally, it seemed that's what they would be doing most often. They'd sit or stand grinning at me while they exhibited themselves. I knew they were trying to get to me psychologically,

Housing for prison personnel, built in 1940 by the WPA, located on the original Army parade ground with San Francisco in the background. *Photo by Barney Peterson, courtesy* San Francisco Chronicle.

and I didn't want to lose control; so I would concentrate on being highly involved with the counts.

The more I tried to ignore them, the cruder they became, until I was forced to threaten to put them on report. Most of the time that put a stop to it—for a while—but then it would start up all over again. Little things like that could get to you after a while. Those kinds of subtle harassments sent many a guard over the edge.

The Towers

I hated working the towers. God, it was monotonous, particularly the midnight-8:00 a.m. shift. It seemed like it was always bitter cold, with chilling winds every night. You couldn't really relax for a moment. Every so often a patrolling lieutenant would signal with a flashlight. If I hadn't signaled back with three flashes, I would have been fired.

I felt very isolated, but at least I was well equipped; I had a Thompson sub-machine gun, a 30-ought-six rifle, a 30-caliber rifle, a tear gas gun, and a 38-revolver. Actually, duty in the gun galleries and in the towers was the only time guards were armed. The rest of the time we had no guns, no clubs, nothing. They did teach us martial arts, but the problem was we practiced on each other. When it came time to use it on the inmates, they weren't quite as cooperative.

I sneaked a radio up to the tower in my lunch bag once and played it real low. But the control center had loud speakers and the music was overheard. The fellow in charge up there told me one morning, "I know you got a radio. Get rid of it." If he had reported me, I would have been suspended for five days. For sleeping on duty, you got fired.

Attention to Detail

The rules and regulations of the prison were read to the convicts as they were brought in, and each new guard received a copy. We had to become accustomed quickly to the restrictions of the institutional routine, and learn to give strict attention to detail. In the words of Alcatraz senior staff: learn to do things the *right* way.

All correctional officers were required to memorize a lot of information: the locations of all gates, towers, rooms, buildings and departments, the rules governing officers, discipline of inmates, daily routines, customers, privileges and restrictions; the daily roll-call, watches, roster and work assignments; the necessity of obedience to orders and the importance of cooperation; how to handle inmates effectively, individually and in groups; how to keep track of inmates at work, in the cellhouse and the yard; how to make out reports on inmates, negative when they misbehaved,

View of road tower, with the guard on duty looking south over the shore line. Located on the west side of the island, the tower was connected to the catwalk around the wall. Towers were manned by 3 shifts, 24 hours a day. *Courtesy Golden Gate National Recreation Area.*

_____19___

United States Penitentiary Watch Call Shee[t]

		6:00	6:30	7:00	7:30	8:00	8:30	9:00	9:30	10:00	10:30	11:00	11:30
Cell House													
Gun Gallery (East)													
Gun Gallery (West)													
Hospital													
Dock & North Island													
Power House													
Road Tower													
Dock Tower													
"D" Block													

FPI INC ERO-5 17-46-800-3176-40

Man on duty

1 _____
2 _____
3 _____
4 _____
5 _____
6 _____
7 _____
8 _____
9 _____

_____
Lieutenant of evening watch

Remarks:

M

1 _____
2 _____
3 _____
4 _____
5 _____
6 _____
7 _____
8 _____
9 _____

_____ 19___

Alcatraz, California

1:30	2:00	2:30	3:00	3:30	4:00	4:30	5:00	5:30	6:00	6:30

_____
Lieutenant of morning watch

Remarks:

Watch Call Sheet. At half hour intervals, all manned gun galleries and towers would call in to indicate that all was well. *Courtesy Larry Quilligan.*

and sometimes positive, commending them for outstanding work or good conduct; how to handle firearms safely; the techniques of self defense; how to maintain control of inmates, without harshness or fraternization.

Contraband, Drugs, and Sex

Warden Swope really stressed the danger of allowing or overlooking contraband—anything smuggled in improperly. No matter how insignificant and harmless a smuggled item might be, once the process started it could lead to serious consequences—to an officer finding himself under pressure from the inmates to bring in other objects, leading eventually to guns, knives, liquor, and drugs.

Alcohol and drugs were minor problems on Alcatraz, mainly because they just weren't as readily available in the general community as they are today. Occasionally, an inmate assigned to the kitchen would take dried fruits—raisins mostly—and ferment them in yeast and water to get high on the juice. And on night duty, when you handed out sleeping pills—"yellow jackets"—even though you tried to make sure they got them down with water, some inmates would cough the pills back up and save them 'till they had enough to try and O.D.

Certainly the worst part of my job was performing the cavity searches. But it was absolutely amazing what some of those inmates could hide. I'm talking about knives, hacksaw blades, pills, cigarettes, even food.

We tried to get a medical technician to do the job whenever we could, but they weren't always available. And any body cavity could conceal some type of material, so we were absolutely forbidden to admit a prisoner to solitary without someone doing a complete body check.

Sex is one of the biggest problems in any prison, and Alcatraz was no exception. Some areas were considered "hot spots," and the hottest was the laundry. Prisoners could conceal themselves—at least for short periods—behind the machinery and in other nooks and crannies.

Another "hot spot" was in the kitchen. There was a basement in the lower kitchen area, and that was usually the place for sexual activity. One of the details I pulled often was as the utility officer—assisting different officers wherever help was needed. Frequently, that meant going down to the laundry or lower kitchen to make sure everyone was behaving himself.

The cons worked in threes, with one guy as the spotter; he'd watch the stairs ready to signal while the other two were going at it. Then they would trade places. I knew what was going on. I heard the signals, the whistles.

Sometimes the sexual activity wasn't so discreet. One time I remember working on the catwalk overlooking the yard. Down in one corner I spotted two fellows fondling each other. They didn't know I'd discovered them. I thought about it, then I turned and walked away.

It just didn't seem that bad to me, and I knew what they would have gone through if I had reported them. I would have had to take them before the trial board and it would have just been my word against the cons'. The warden probably would have taken my side, but I didn't want to go through the ordeal, and I didn't want them to have to either.

If any of the inmates had seen me, it would have been different. I would have been forced to write them up, because otherwise they would classify you as an "easy mark," and, once you got that reputation, the prisoners would never let up on you.

The shower room was also a favorite—and a natural—sexual spot. The years I worked there we had stall showers, and the inmates could easily conceal themselves. It was also one of the worst duties you could pull. I saw fistfights and knifings. There were murders and beatings. I still have nightmares about some of the things I saw.

I remember a fellow I met in D-Block, the isolation or "special treatment" unit. I was working the night shift, four to twelve midnight. This guy was always bragging that he was the greatest lover on Alcatraz Island. One time he told me he had had his lover friend inside his shower stall and they had gotten it on while I was "...only six feet away, and you didn't know anything about it." He thought that was a riot. It wasn't a riot when he finally got caught; that's why he was in solitary.

After I had been on the job only a few months, I realized the inherent—and inevitable—danger of my position. I stopped being naive and started thinking, "What the hell have I gotten myself into?" But I felt I'd asked for it and I had to stick it out. I didn't want to go back and say I couldn't take it. Saving face was more important.

Dealing with the Crazies

I got asked so many times: "You were so young. You must have had a lot of problems among those desperate men. What kind of problems did you have?" My answer has often been that the worst times were when inmates went off the deep end.

You never knew for sure whether a prisoner who started acting crazy had really gone off the deep end, or whether he was putting on an act. There was a reason to give the impression you'd broken down mentally. The ultimate goal was to be judged insane and sent to Springfield, Missouri. Springfield in the Federal system is the prison hospital (like Vacaville is in the California state system).

Often an inmate would start acting out in his cell—to the point where taking these apparent nuts out of their cells became a recurring problem. But I remember my first experience with it—about a month after I started to work.

It was very typical. The inmate was inside his cell, hollering and screaming, and so a lieutenant, another officer, and I came over. The inmate glared at us and issued an invitation to come on in (using a lot of four letter words—which was not unusual). My adrenalin was way up. I knew that this prisoner just wanted to get us—to get a piece of us.

It's scary anyway, but particularly the first time when you're not really sure what to do. Well I found out right away, because the lieutenant looked at me and said, "Mr. Heaney, I want you to go in first." I couldn't quite understand that, because I thought the most experienced guy would go in first. But I also knew that you do not question a lieutenant.

I found out that he had a good reason, though, a very good reason. When he sent me in that cell, the inmate grabbed me and threw me against the side of it. And when his back was turned momentarily, the lieutenant stepped in and hit him in the back of the head with a blackjack. He went down the first time, and we put a straitjacket on him and took him away.

Later the lieutenant came and told me that I had been used as a "diversionary tactic." Actually it had worked well, because we got the fellow down fast. I've been in those cells at other times when we weren't quite so lucky. They are very small—only 5 X 7 X 9, and you couldn't get very many people in them at a time. (You'd never go in alone, though, without someone to back you up.) I've been in there up to 10 minutes getting injured trying to drag an inmate out.

You couldn't just leave the guy in there. The other inmates were always right on the edge, too, and the noise would start them going. They'd take their cups and ring them up and down on the bars, start hollering, and if you let them keep it up, they'd start lighting their cells on fire.

The Bars

Guards would go along and check every bar on every man's cell with a rubber mallet. If a bar had a different sound to it when it was tapped, you knew someone had been trying to file it down.

New bars had been installed in 1934, with two layers of different metals*: the outside layer was all casehard, inside and out, but inside was a round steel bar. Even if a prisoner did hacksaw through the outer layer, when he got to the inside, his blade would just go 'round and 'round.

But it didn't take long for the inmates to figure out what to do about that: They stole pieces of metal from the machine shop and jammed them between two bars to hold the inside firm while they sawed away on the outer layer. Then they'd take the filings, blend them with dark paint, and smear it on to cover cut marks. Still, no one ever escaped through those bars.

*We were told that combinations of metals were used; a sample bar was examined after the prison closed, and was found to be solid steel.

The second kind of bar we installed had molten lead inside. There was simply no way anyone could cut through it with a hacksaw—or a cutting torch for that matter. Still, the inmates tried, and so we had to have shakedowns. In fact, the administration was so concerned about it that they would make test cuts to see if the guards reported them on their rounds. If the cuts weren't noticed, we were subject to severe disciplinary action.

Disciplinary Measures

Punishment was progressive. If it was a minor infraction, the first time a prisoner would just be warned. The second time, he would be denied the privilege of going out into the yard on weekends, or he might lose his job. It built up. The worst punishment, probably worse than solitary for some, was to have "good time" taken away.

"Good time" was time taken off a man's sentence for good behavior. If you were a particulary cooperative inmate, you could get five or ten days off a month, plus maybe another five or ten days if you were working in one of the prison industries. You could presumably get your sentence reduced by as much as fifty percent for serving good time. As you can imagine, this was quite an incentive for an inmate to keep his act straight.

Any privilege could easily be taken away by the warden, the associate warden, or the captain.

Running the Movies

All inmates were usually reasonably well behaved when a movie was playing because other inmates would get mad if a movie were stopped. But we did have a knifing or a fistfight sometimes. The east gun gallery overlooked it all, and we had an armed guard covering us with a 30-caliber rifle and a 38-revolver at all times; we were not allowed to have weapons down there.

Our families were sometimes allowed to watch the movies at night in a segregated area of the same room as the inmates. (There was a way to get up in the top area without going through the cellhouse.) Inmates would walk through a special gate in the inside; the entryway that the families would take was in the main corridor and through the administration wing. I would go on up there and watch with the families or go down to the officers club, our entertainment area.

Visitors

Although visiting Alcatraz was very difficult and definitely not encouraged, we did have our share of guests: FBI agents, officials,

Visitors talking to inmates. They talked via telephone, separated by a glass partition. They could discuss family business only—conversations were monitored by prison guards. Infractions could bring severe punishment, such as solitary confinement. *Courtesy Golden Gate National Recreation Area.*

judges, movie stars like Howard Duff, Robert Taylor, and John Sutton, senators, congressmen, police chiefs—anyone thought to have some influence with the Department of Justice could more than likely have a tour.

Prisoners were allowed one one-and-a-half-hour-visit once a month. If you had a visitor coming from a long distance, most often you were allowed a back-to-back visit, which meant they could come on the last day of the month and the first day of the next. This is what May Capone (Al's wife) did, since she lived in Miami.

Sick Call

Illnesses were exaggerated. Sick call was every day after the noon meal, and there was always a long line. I'd estimate ten percent of the prison population showed up daily. The first attendant they would see was the medical technician. He would give them a routine check, and maybe a doctor would prescribe sleeping pills, the drug they usually asked for; yellow-jackets were a favorite.

Many were in line *every day*. Maybe it was just to have something to do. Going up and bellyaching to a doctor took some of the boredom away, or relieved the pressure of monotony.

We had a great staff doctor, Richard Yocom, the commander in the public health service. He lived on the island in a beautiful home on the top of the hill next to the warden's house. (He lives not too far from me today.) We also had doctors on call from the public health hospital in San Francisco.

There was a dentist, a psychiatrist, and several specialists who came over periodically. We had a fully accredited hospital with a large treatment room, x-ray and operating rooms, a psychiatric ward, and several sick rooms where ill prisoners could be kept for short periods. If an inmate had a long-term illness, he would generally be sent to the prison hospital at Springfield, Missouri.

Nicknames

I used to love to listen to jazz. On Sundays they would play the corniest music in the yard, and I'd complain about it. Of course the inmates didn't know any different because they were rather out of touch. One day, a guy asked me what was popular in music now and I said they were mostly playing bebop—a kind of upbeat from swing... progressive music. So from that time on I was nicknamed "Bebop."

That nickname actually could have hurt me. It would have been bad news if a superior had heard them calling me that; it just sounded too friendly. Particularly when a lot of the other officers had worse names—like "fat ass," or "turd breath."

NOTORIOUS PRISONERS

Machine Gun Kelly

When I first met George "Machine Gun" Kelly, he had already been on Alcatraz for fourteen years; he had been in the first group of convicts transferred from Leavenworth in 1934. He once told me that if he had committed his most famous crime—the Urschel kidnapping—after the Lindbergh case, he would never have been on Alcatraz; he would have been executed. It's been said that Kelly made the FBI's most wanted list because J. Edgar Hoover wanted to make an example of him, to gain publicity for the Bureau.

Kelly was from Memphis, Tennessee. His father was a prosperous insurance agent and Kelly had had a good upbringing, with a college education. He was a very distinguished-looking man. Of course, all of the inmates had to wear prison coveralls, but Kelly's were always impeccable, with his chambray shirt perfectly creased. He was about 5'10" with a medium build, maybe just a little bit heavy. He had kind of a ruddy complexion and, I believe, hazel eyes. He had a thin nose and full lips—a nice looking fellow with a ready smile.

Kelly served as the altar boy at the Catholic services, and also as the projectionist for the movies. He was somewhat shy at first with those he didn't know, but after a while he tended to warm up; and he did to me, maybe because we were both Irishmen. He really was a nice fellow, and reminded me more of a bank president than a bank robber.

Kelly told me he first got involved in his life of crime being a runner for a bootlegger, the kid that runs the booze between the bootlegger and the customer. Later on, he advanced to being the bootlegger himself. Then he met Kate Shannon, the beautiful mistress of the biggest rum runner in Oklahoma. He fell madly in love with her right before he was sentenced to three years in Leavenworth for bootlegging. They were married as soon as he got out.

With the hard times of the Depression, and through contacts he had made in Leavenworth, Kelly soon found himself involved in more serious activities, leading to a sensational kidnapping. His victim, Charles Urschel, was a millionaire from Oklahoma.

Above: George R. "Machine Gun" Kelly in his earlier years. *Courtesy National Maritime Museum, San Francisco.*

Opposite: The capture of Alvin Karpis by J. Edgar Hoover's men in New Orleans, May, 1936. *Courtesy National Maritime Museum, San Francisco.*

Opposite, top: Harvey Bailey, an escape artist, here shown handcuffed and hobbled with chains after escaping from Dallas County Jail. *Courtesy National Maritime Museum.*

Opposite, bottom: Kathryn and George "Machine Gun" Kelly, standing during their joint trial as sentence was pronounced for the kidnapping of Charles Urschel in Oklahoma City, in 1933. *Courtesy National Maritime Museum, San Francisco.*

Kelly admired him a great deal, for his cunning and for his intelligence—even though these traits brought his downfall. (That's when he changed his name from Barnes to Kelly—his mother's maiden name—so as not to bring disgrace on the family.)

George spoke freely and openly to me about the kidnapping. He seemed sincere, and I believed him. He said he had grown tired of bank robberies, that they they were penny-ante stuff. He and his wife Kate decided that, if they could just get enough money, they could get out of crime for good. And so they planned this one big job—for a $200,000 ransom. There is no way of telling what would have happened if they had pulled it off.

I think his story was sensationalized to an extreme. He was not one to brag about his life; in fact, he felt very foolish and stupid about many of the things he had done. I believe he sincerely would rather have gone straight. I guess that's what they all say, but I tended to believe him more than any of the other prisoners. I honestly think he could have been very successful in the conventional world; he was very intelligent and very engaging. He just took the wrong path and wound up in prison.

In 1933, Kelly and Albert Bates, a burglar, safecracker, and fellow bank robber, broke into the Urschel home and surprised Urschel, his wife, and another couple. Kelly didn't know which one was Urschel, so he first took both men, but when Urschel revealed his identity, they let the other man go.

Urschel was bound, gagged, and blindfolded, and driven across the Oklahoma border into Texas. There he was locked inside an old wooden shed next to the farmhouse of Kelly's father-in-law, Boss Shannon, and kept while the ransom message was delivered. Boss Shannon was kind of a hick politician of that area—anything illegal going on, he was probably in the middle of it. Kelly and other gang members used to hang out there.

Although she'd been warned not to, Urschel's wife had immediately notified the FBI and local police. The money was dropped at a predetermined spot and Urschel was released. Then the search began.

Although Kelly had warned him that his family would be put in real danger or possibly killed if he did, Urschel went straight to the police. He proved amazingly helpful in the search for the kidnappers. He remembered many small details associated with the kidnapping and his imprisonment. Although he had been blindfolded the entire time (except when he was allowed to write the ransom note), he had paid special attention to smells, sounds, and tastes.

Urschel had been aware of crossing the state line, and he knew he had been taken to a rural area from the sounds of the horses and cows on the farm. He noticed during his captivity that every day a plane flew overhead, and, a short time later, he would ask for the time. (He even thought to ask at different times every day, so as not to arouse suspicion.) One day, the plane didn't come by, and he made a mental note of that, too. Most interestingly, Urschel remembered the taste of the water, and supposed that it was some kind of well water.

After his release, when the FBI heard these accounts, they inmmediately ran a check on the times of mail flights over Texas. It didn't take long to locate a flight which had been diverted one day because of bad weather. They plotted the plane's route, and narrowed down the general target area to the vicinity of Paris, Texas, home of Kate's parents.

FBI agents then disguised themselves as farmers and salesmen and started combing the area asking questions. They soon reduced their search to Kelly's father-in-law's ranch. They brought water samples to Urschel and he identified the one from the ranch by the taste he remembered.

Urschel and the FBI agents went out to the ranch and checked it over. Shannon, Kelly's father-in-law, was arrested, along with one poor sucker who was really in the wrong place at the wrong time: Harvey Bailey, a fellow wanted for murder in the Kansas City Massacre. (Funny thing about it, he eventually wound up on Alcatraz, too.)

Kelly and his wife had fled. They went on the lam for two months with the FBI on their tail, traveling throughout the Midwest, then the South and finally to Tennessee. He said one of the toughest times in his life was that two-month period after the kidnapping, when he was being chased by the FBI.

Fifty-six days from the date of the kidnapping, the FBI traced them to a Memphis bungalow and went in to make the arrest. The story goes that Kelly put up his hands and said, "Don't shoot, G-Men!" but Kelly himself has no recollection of making that statement. They were brought to trial and convicted. Kate and her mother both wound up in a Federal penitentiary. Her father was sent to Leavenworth, and Kelly went to Alcatraz with a life sentence.

From time to time, I remember, the FBI would come over to Alcatraz to question "Machine Gun." He allegedly knew about some of the ransom money that had not been returned. He refused to tell them anything, and I think that had something to do with his deportment status. That and the fact that he had really blown it when he had sent a letter to Urschel saying, "Just a few lines to let you know that I'm getting my plans laid to destroy you, your so-called mansion, and your family immediately after the trial. If you don't get the government off my back, I'll see you in hell." Kelly also sent threatening letters to the prosecuting attorneys, to the judge himself—even to Hoover—during his trial.

That was always surprising to me, almost as if it couldn't have been the same person I knew. As far as I could tell, he was one of the most stable prisoners on the island. Kelly never seemed to down-grade anyone. He wasn't like a lot of them who always blamed someone else. He wasn't bitter about things, and recognized that it was his own fault that he was on Alcatraz.

But I guess Kelly's record worked against him and kept him on Alcatraz. He finally left in the 1950s for Leavenworth, where his luck ran out: he died of a heart attack on July 17, 1954—his 59th birthday.

Floyd Hamilton

George Kelly and Floyd Hamilton had a couple of things in common. For one, there was a strong similarity to the patterns of their holdups. They'd each start by picking a remote area—remember, this was back in the late '20s and '30s when communications were more primitive, and many towns were truly isolated.

They'd go into a town and stay maybe one or two days and case the place. They'd learn the habits of the local police. They'd have one or two accomplices in charge of cutting off the radio station, they'd make sure the local law enforcement officials were out of the way, and then they'd simply cut the telegraph and telephone wires. Two way radios were not yet in common use. The town literally would be cut off from the rest of the world while they were robbing the bank, and they would get away easily. Once they crossed the state line, they were home free. There were no hot-pursuit laws in those days.

Kelly and Hamilton seemed to hit it off right from the start. They happened to become the two projectionists on Alcatraz. (You needed an inmate for each of the two 35mm cameras.) There was an officer in the back watching them the whole time, but they had a lot of chances to talk. I'm sure they had a lot of similar memories.

Floyd Hamilton was most famous as the driver for Bonnie and Clyde. He told me that they had all grown up as kids together in Dallas, Texas, where Clyde's father had had a gas station. Floyd said Clyde was a reclusive sort; he wouldn't hang out with other kids. Bonnie, on the other hand, was as outgoing a girl as you could find.

Floyd was about 5'10", maybe 6' tall. He seemed a nice enough fellow to me—just a down-home Texas boy. He told me he liked the food better in Texas prisons, but otherwise preferred being on Alcatraz. What he didn't like was the lack of privileges. He said that at times he could even have accepted the sadistic guards in Texas, just to get away from the constant monotony of "the Rock."

It all had started when Clyde got into trouble at about age eighteen and was put in prison for a couple of years. When he got out, the three of them—Bonnie, Clyde, and Floyd—hooked up and started staging bank robberies. Floyd's brother, Ray, was a driver for them sometimes, too. (Ray wound up in the Texas electric chair.)

Floyd told me, "In the Midwest, once you start holding up banks, you might as well keep it up. How do you stop, with the law after you all the time?" He said all he wanted to do in the end was stay alive. In a sense he did, but of course he was alive on Alcatraz.

I had many opportunities to talk with him when I worked night shift in D-Block. He was always locked up in there—isolation—punishment for his escape attempt, which he described in detail to me.

Ray Hamilton, brother of Floyd Hamilton and also a driver for Bonnie and Clyde, with Clyde Barrow. Ray was executed in the electric chair in Texas. *Courtesy Golden Gate National Recreation Area.*

Upper: Bodies of Bonnie and Clyde in the morgue. *Courtesy Golden Gate National Recreation Area.*

Lower: The car in which Clyde Barrow and Bonnie Parker were riding when taken by the posse. *Courtesy Golden Gate National Recreation Area.*

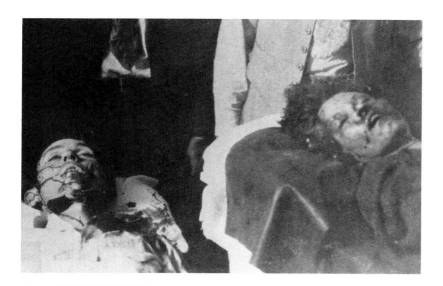

Members of the posse who ambushed Bonnie and Clyde. *Courtesy Golden Gate National Recreation Area.*

It had been in 1944, and he had made the attempt with three other inmates—Harold Brest, Fred Hunter, and James Boarman. They started in the model shop area of Alcatraz, the industrial section built by the army on the northern part of the island. Armed with homemade knives, they jumped one officer, and first trussed him up; then Officer Smith, a friend of mine, came in. They jumped him, too, tied him up, and escaped through a window.

They headed down the shoreline towards San Francisco where they had hidden some stolen army uniforms sealed up in cans. Floyd thought they wouldn't be noticed in uniform in San Francisco, with so many military men from the war.

Well, they were spotted by Frank Roberts, an officer in the model shop tower (and another good friend of mine). Unfortunately for the inmates, Frank was a very good shot. They were scouting for cans to use as floats when Frank opened fire. The four of them jumped onto the cans, shoved out from shore, and tried to get out of range. Boarman was hit and apparently killed, and his body slid into the bay, never to be found. Hunter was found hidden in a cave, and Brest was captured in the water.

But Hamilton was hiding in back of the rocks and they couldn't see him. He figured if he could get behind the riprap boulders they used to stop tidal erosion, he could hide until he could make his attempt to cross to San Francisco. But, after two days, he got tired and hungry and decided he'd never make it. So he snuck back up on the island, and they found him, sent him to the hospital, and then put him in D-Block where I got to talk to him so much.

I understand that when he finally was released in 1958, he did straighten out. In fact, he became a born-again Christian. Floyd Hamilton died in 1984 in Dallas after a long illness.

Clarence Carnes

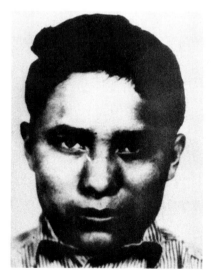

Clarence Carnes. *Courtesy National Maritime Museum, San Francisco.*

Clarence Carnes was a full-blooded Chocktaw Indian from Oklahoma and only eighteen years old (the same age as I) when he was sent to Alcatraz; he was the youngest inmate.

He wasn't quite as talkative as some of the other inmates but we did have some interesting conversations. He told me about his family on the reservation, and how much he regretted, for their sake, getting involved in crime. He said he was just a crazy kid and maybe if he'd had a closer relationship with his parents he wouldn't have turned out so bad.

He had started the way most prisoners had—getting involved in petty crimes, then working his up to a murder/robbery with another kid. He was in prison in Oklahoma when he made his first escape, stealing a car and its two occupants. When he drove it across the state line, he automatically committed two Federal crimes: kidnapping and car theft across a state line. That mistake, coupled with the fact that he was always getting into fights with other inmates, was enough to get him on Alcatraz.

Clarence was kept in the D-Block area most of the time because of his involvement in the 1946 blastout.

Charles Berta

Another inmate I remember quite well was Charles Berta, one of the first inmates transferred from Leavenworth when Alcatraz opened in 1934. Originally sentenced for robbing a post office, Berta had been sent to the Rock because of an escape attempt. He and six fellow inmates had captured the warden and made their way out of the prison area, but in the process they had triggered the alarm system and were caught.

Berta was an exception to the general policy of not releasing prisoners directly from Alcatraz. He went out the front door with no holds on him. He left in 1949, about a year after I started working there. I still remember the day we took him down to be fitted for his "going away" suit. He was really nervous and I can understand why: the guy had spent twenty-four years behind bars. Some of the inmates smuggled yellow-jackets in to calm him down, and by the time he checked out, he was feeling no pain.

From what I understand, he went to San Francisco, became a bartender, and completely straightened out.

Creepy Karpis

Alvin "Creepy" Karpis was convicted of shooting down a policeman in Kansas and kidnapping William Hamm, the brewery millionaire. He got between $100,000-$150,000 in ransom. He also claimed to have pulled off quite a few bank robberies. It was always difficult to know the real truth; you heard things from so many sources, but I do believe he was definitely on the fast track.

When he had been declared Public Enemy #1, he knew his time was really running out. He tried to get his fingerprints removed, and he had plastic surgery on his face, but the job was botched by a quack doctor. Karpis' real waterloo was kidnapping the president of a Minnesota bank. He got a $200,000 ransom—all in marked bills—and he was easily traced to a house in New Orleans.

There are two versions to the story of his final capture. This was said to be the only arrest J. Edgar Hoover, director of the FBI, ever made. The official version given to the public was that Hoover flew down to New Orleans after being told that Karpis was holed up there in an apartment, and made the arrest personally.

Upper: Mug shot of Alvin "Creepy" Karpis. *Courtesy Golden Gate National Recreation Area.*

Lower: Alvin Karpis leaving the McNeil Island Penitentiary after serving 33 years for kidnapping. *Courtesy National Maritime Museum, San Francisco.*

But Karpis told *me* that Hoover was actually hiding behind a building. And that it was only after his agents had gone in and captured Karpis that Hoover appeared, to take credit. You can believe whichever version you like, but I've met many FBI agents since then who tend to agree with Karpis' story.

Karpis used to talk about the notorious Ma Barker. The tales I heard about her varied, depending upon the inmate telling the story. Many recalled her as a morally loose woman, and I don't really know if she ever married. It was also said that she was the one who taught her boys how to use firearms.

Creepy Karpis spoke differently about her. He said she was just a woman devoted to her offspring, her "boys," and she merely followed them around. (Freddy was her favorite son; Doc was sent to Alcatraz where he was later shot and killed.) He said she always wanted to be cooking for them and helping them out—apparently she took him in and accepted him as one of her own.

Karpis said Ma didn't plan to get involved in the crimes in any way, but his story doesn't equate very well with the circumstances of her death—in Florida with a Thompson submachine gun in her hand.

Karpis served 26 years on Alcatraz, the longest of any prisoner. Eventually he was transferred to McNeil Island, and finally paroled to his home in Canada. Rumor has it that years later he committed suicide somewhere in Spain.

The Nazis

We actually had three Nazi spies among our prisoners in the late '40s. They were part of about a dozen Nazis who had landed from a U-boat in 1942 off the coast of Florida. They were saboteurs, commissioned to blow up American war plants. The Coast Guard was alerted to the threat, and mounted a massive search for them, and apparently they were all caught. I do know that some were executed, and three wound up on Alcatraz. Once there, none of them wanted anything to do with the others.

One Nazi was in D-Block. He was pretty nutty; he didn't communicate, went around naked, wouldn't eat, and was skinny as a rail. Another was named Heindrick, and he wasn't much brighter. He had been caught in Chicago when the taxicab he was in was stopped for speeding. When they were pulled over, Heindrick immediately surrendered to the cops, so you can see how smart he was.

The oldest of the three wasn't too bad. I talked with him many times and he would tell me about his wife back in Germany, whom he missed very much. He had been born in the United States, but had been taken to Germany at a very early age, and eventually recruited for the sabotage assignment.

You'd expect that, being a Nazi spy, he would have been ostracized by the American inmates; but they really didn't pay that much attention to him. He never bothered anyone—he just talked

Arthur "Doc" Barker in county jail after receiving life sentence for kidnapping, May 1935. *Courtesy National Maritime Museum, San Francisco.*

about getting out of Alcatraz and going back to Germany, which I'm sure he did in the late '50s.

Murder Incorporated

One prisoner who worked in the kitchen was apparently a mobster in the Murder Incorporated Gang. He was constantly after me for fig bars. Whatever his past, he was a neat guy to talk to. He told me about his job as a member of the gang—he was the maker of cement shoes. The way he told it to me was that at first, if someone had taken a contract out on a person, a member of the Gang had simply taken the "target" out into the country, finished him off, and disposed of the evidence.

But sometimes the bodies had been found, often dug up by dogs or other animals, and so they had had to come up with another system. The solution was to convert a warehouse into a "cement shoe factory." They'd prop a body up with its feet in wash pails, fill the pails with cement and let it harden, then dump the corpse off a pier, and that was the end of it—fish food. If half of this guy's stories were true, there are a lot of wash pails at the bottom of the Hudson River.

Harmon Waley

About a year or so after the Lindbergh kidnapping, the heir to the Weyerhauser lumber millions was kidnapped in Tacoma, Washington.

One of his kidnappers was Harmon Waley, a prisoner I knew quite well from the band room, where he spent a lot of time. He was kind of a morose fellow, very depressed about the time he had to serve in solitary confinement.

It was quite a kidnapping case in its day, and there were articles about it in all the papers. Waley had taken the young boy from his home and buried him alive for a period of time in some sort of coffin. Then he had kept him in a secluded farmhouse while he sent a ransom note asking for $200,000. (That seemed to be the going rate.)

The money was paid, but the family had notified the FBI and all the bills were marked. The first one arrested was Waley, along with his wife. Because of the severity of the crime, he was sent to McNeil Island and later transferred to Alcatraz. Funny thing, I heard Harmon went back to work for Weyerhauser after being released.

(Another fellow involved in the kidnapping, Daynard, eventually wound up on Alcatraz too. He was never as talkative as Waley, but then a lot of the prisoners were cautious about that; they didn't want to be known as a stoolie—someone too friendly with the guards.)

Upper: Guard and Harmon M. Waley getting out of car, at courthouse in Tacoma, Washington, July 1935. *Courtesy National Maritime Museum, San Francisco.*

Lower: Basil "The Owl" Banghart. *Courtesy National Maritime Museum, San Francisco.*

Roy Gardner

In 1939 my parents and I had gone to Treasure Island, for the World's Fair, Pan American Pacific Exposition. There was an exhibit there that had always stuck in my memory (right next to Sally Rand's Nude Ranch). It was a live show starring a former inmate of Alcatraz, Roy Gardner—a well-known escape artist, bank robber, mail train thief, and general all-around flamboyant person.

He had been one of the last great train robbers and jewel thieves. He had been as famous as Al Capone or Machine Gun Kelly at the time. Maybe even more so because he was also an escape artist as well as Public Enemy #1; in fact, that's one of the reasons he ended up in the tight security of the Rock.

The name of his show was "Crime Doesn't Pay," and Roy had lots of very graphic pictures. Unfortunately, he had a lot of competition in the carnival-like atmosphere of the World's Fair, and his program was cancelled.

When his exhibit folded, Roy was quite distraught. He had tried conventional jobs and couldn't stand the routine, even though he had become a model prisoner on Alcatraz. As the story goes, Roy went to a hotel room in San Francisco one night, dropped a couple of cyanide pellets in a glass of acid (the way it's done in executions on San Quentin), covered his head with a towel, and breathed in the fumes. When the maid came by to make her rounds, she noticed a note on the door that read, "Do Not Open This Door. Poison Gas. Call Police." He was a gentleman to the end.

He had packed his luggage neatly and stacked it in the corner. On top was a fifty-cent tip for the maid. The combined loot from his robberies had been reported to be several hundred thousand dollars, but he left only $3.69.

His suicide note said he was just old and tired and didn't care to struggle any more. It said to "let him down as light as possible." Roy was the type that loved the limelight more than anything else. When he couldn't get back to the glitter of society, he went out with a flourish. He set his own stage and his own tragic final scene.

Basil Banghart

One prisoner, Basil "The Owl" Banghart (with his large head and big eyes he kind of looked like one), had been sentenced to ninety-nine years for kidnapping. At the same time he had been given a Federal sentence of thirty-six years for mail robbery. He had been involved with another notorious criminal named Roger Touhy in another prison where they had smuggled in guns, shot a guard, and escaped. The FBI got involved because of the Federal sentences, and that's why he was sent to Alcatraz.

Banghart was very astute and alert; he had quite a high intellect, just not too many scruples. I'd put him in the same class as "Creepy" Karpis. Above all else, felt he was a professional man; he thought his occupation was being a crook, and Banghart felt the same way.

John Paul Chase

George "Baby Face" Nelson, who was killed in a shoot-out with the FBI while with John Paul Chase (who escaped but was later captured and sent to Alcatraz). *Courtesy Golden Gate National Recreation Area.*

Some of the inmates were very good artists—John Paul Chase, for example, whom I remember quite well. He had been involved with Baby Face Nelson in the murder of an FBI agent. He worked in the prison industries as a cobbler, and was put in my charge (along with two inmates who worked as dry cleaners). They were older and easy to handle.

Father Clark, our Catholic chaplain, first got him interested in painting and, at one time, there was an art instructor who came over from San Francisco to teach the formal techniques of painting. He had paintings displayed and often sold them, so evidently he was quite good. Of course he had a lot of time to learn.

Cecil Wright

Cecil Wright was one of the most famous cellhouse lawyers. Cecil had pulled so many guys out of Leavenworth on writs of habeas corpus that they sent him to Alcatraz. Once there, he started doing the same thing.

It had all started in 1930 when the State of Illinois had imprisoned him for holding up a poker game, and robbing a post office of $2.43. When he was sent to Leavenworth he argued and won his own case—twice!

But Wright had grown accustomed to life in jail, and the outside world seemed too challenging. For years he was in and out of Federal penitentiaries, pleading guilty to crimes he later said he never really committed, until his final release in 1982. Cecil had reviewed over 400 inmates' cases by the time he left prison life.

Al Capone

Al Capone was the most famous of the prisoners originally transferred from Atlanta in 1934. However, the strict rules of Alcatraz reduced him to just another inmate, and he was actually a sick man, with irreversible brain damage from syphillis. Eventually he was transferred to Terminal Island in Southern California, later released, and died at his family estate in Miami in 1947.

Robert Stroud ("The Birdman of Alcatraz")

Robert Stroud, the Birdman, first got in trouble in Alaska during the time of the Gold Strike, right after the turn of the century. He killed a man in a bar room brawl.

Now there are different versions of that story—some said he was a pimp and got in a fight over one of his girls—somebody

Robert Stroud, the "Birdman" of Alcatraz, June 1958. *Courtesy National Maritime Museum, San Francisco.*

didn't pay, or... There are different versions, but he definitely did kill a man in Alaska.

He was convicted of manslaughter, which got him sent to McNeil Island. While at McNeil he was a very violent, volatile sort of man, and he had a lot of problems. Among other things, he stabbed an inmate six times—that apparently provided his ticket to Leavenworth.

While serving his time at Leavenworth, he was looking forward to a visit from his mother, which was suddenly cancelled. Because of some minor infraction, he had been put on report and had lost his visiting privileges—and he was seething. He got hold of some sort of sharp implement, smuggled it into the dining hall and stabbed the officer who had put him on report, killing him in the dining hall in front of all the inmates.

He was convicted of murder and sentenced to hang. They had to build a gallows because the state of Kansas where this happened did not have any execution chambers. (The Federal Government's policy is to use state execution facilities.) While they were building the gallows, Stroud's mother was pleading for clemency, first with President Wilson; when she couldn't persuade him directly, she went to Mrs. Wilson and pleaded with her. She persuaded her to take a document commuting the sentence to the President, who was apparently by then ailing and not very alert. He signed it, and Robert Stroud was sentenced to life imprisonment without possibility of parole.

This made the prison officals very angry. To make it as tough on him as possible, they went by the original sentence, which had said that he must remain in isolation until his execution. So Robert Stroud remained in complete isolation for forty-four years (fifty-fours years total in jail). As far as we know, this was the longest term of any inmate in complete isolation.

He got his birds at Leavenworth. It began when he found a small sparrow out in his little exercise area. He brought it into his cell and nursed it, and began to develop an interest in birds. He found other birds and did the same thing, became increasingly interested, and started corresponding with different bird societies, asking for information.

He started experimenting, dissecting birds that died; and the bird societies kept sending him more information. He made sketches of various types of birds, and gradually added to his knowledge. (Eventually he wrote *Stroud's Digest of the Diseases of Birds*, which is still on library shelves.)

Over the years the story of Stroud and his birds began to pose problems for the Leavenworth prison authorities. Other inmates wanted birds, cats or dogs. ("If Stroud can have them why can't we? We want to do some research, too.")

And Stroud was a natural trouble-maker. He was allegedly distilling alcohol out of bird seed, making bird cages with false bottoms that he used to smuggle things in and out of the prison. He had a business, an actual business. He'd make these bird cages and other things, and he'd sell them on the outside to keep his business going.

For years they had wanted to send him to Alcatraz, but he held them off by getting the bird societies to put pressure on the prison administration to keep him at Leavenworth. But with the beginning of World War II, peoples' thoughts were not so much on Robert Stroud and his problems; along with the population generally, the birdwatchers in effect went to war. The prison administration took advantage of the situation. They woke him up in the middle of the night and bundled him off without his birds.

Arriving at Alcatraz in 1942, he was put in D-Block, the special treatment unit. He stayed there until about the time I started working there, in 1948, when he was transferred to the prison hospital. He stayed there until 1959—after I had left.

I had occasion to take Stroud into his bath on more than one occasion after he had been moved to the prison hospital. I was of course very young, but I must admit that he made me nervous. His prison record reflected that he had been an active homosexual during his prior imprisonment (though not, so far as we knew, at Alcatraz), and he had a way of looking at someone like me that seemed very suggestive. His insistence on shaving every hair off of his body did not help me to feel that he was normal.

His IQ was 134 and he could read and write in three or four languages. But he was psychotic, subject to severe up and down swings in his moods. In the main, his moods were not too good, but he did have his rational times. He could be very rational when he wanted to be—when he would seek information from me about what was going on in the outside world.

He never had any birds on Alcatraz, but they still called him the Birdman of Alcatraz. It made good copy when they wrote a book and made a movie about him—much better than "The Birdman of Leavenworth."

The Prisoner Mentality

A frightening statistic I learned early on was that seventy-five percent of the prisoners on Alcatraz were deemed psycopathic. That didn't mean they were a group of raving lunatics, but it did mean we had to be extremely careful in dealing with them.

One of their characteristics—even though they were generally very individualistic—was always to act in unison under pressure. If there was an escape attempt, or a disruption of any sort, they would all try to join in, hang together, whatever you want to call it.

Even those declared severe psychopaths often had extremely high intelligence scores. Inmates often looked normal and had excellent vocabularies. At the same time, they usually showed poor judgment and lack of self control, and they were all definitely self-centered.

Rarely could an inmate find fault with his own actions. They felt very much victimized. It was always others, someone else that they blamed.

FINAL MORNING EXTRA

San Francisco Chronicle
The City's Only Home-Owned Newspaper

FOUNDED 1865—VOL. CLXII, NO. 108 — CCCCAAAB — SAN FRANCISCO, FRIDAY, MAY 3, 1946 — DAILY 5 CENTS, SUNDAY 15 CENTS

COMPARATIVE TEMPERATURES

	High	Low		High	Low
San Francisco	58	48	New York	74	54
Oakland	59	49	Chicago	68	54
Los Angeles	69	55	New Orleans	83	68
Sacramento	71	46	Washington	69	61
Seattle	81	47	Salt Lake City	73	35
Reno	80	28	Pensacola	74	72

THIS WORLD TODAY
By ROYCE BRIER

SENATOR ELLENDER of Louisiana is one of Huey Long's boys. He was a floor leader in Huey's personal legislature, and two years after the assassination he was still telling what a wonderful little guy Huey was, and singing the virtue of the Long kind of dictatorship.

Aside from that—which will place him for you in case you have forgotten—Ellender is just another run-of-the-mill Southern statesman of the Claghorne brand, not as obnoxious to sensible men as Bilbo, but without much to recommend him but his set of prejudices. These are pretty gaudy, being compounded of ignorance-of-the-subject, gall-to-attack-it-anyway, isolationism and a full quota of sectional obsessions.

This man has proved in a hundred speeches that he knows very little history (excepting that of the Lower Mississippi, 1861-1946), very little about how and why peoples act in the mass, and very little of the problems besetting the modern world, particularly the problems besetting Europe. His speeches reveal that he follows a reactionary line at home, and abroad a vague-anti-foreign line, which he and those of like mind find synonymous with "pro-American," a term they use repeatedly. Brooks of Illinois let it float on the breeze only yesterday.

But Ellender is a very important man in the affairs of the United States out in the world. As a member of your Senate, he has one-ninety-sixth of the say as to whether we will have a decent and stable future, or another and more massive dose of the chaos we have been enjoying for a third of a century. Consequently his words are worth weighing when he gets on his feet to face an issue like the proposed British loan.

Ellender is against the loan. That is his right, and is not particularly interesting. What is interesting is his reasoning or belief in the matter.

He says Britain is a "dead horse" which can't be revived, and that $3,750,000,000 would be only a "shot in the arm."

"To keep Britain in her trade position," he avers, "we will have to keep pouring money into London like pouring water into a rat-hole."

He went on to say Britain is past the point where the islands can maintain a large population by selling manufactured goods to
Continued on Page 4, Col. 1

ALCATRAZ SIEGE!
Photos of Prisoners' Rebellion! One Guard Killed, 16 Injured

YOU ARE WATCHING the battle of Alcatraz from a boat only 100 yards off the island in San Francisco bay. The three men in the circles below are penitentiary guards who have just fired long-range through the barred cell block windows to smash the glass. Now the guards along the catwalk, half way up the wall, are crouching for momentary safety, then reaching on tiptoe to fire bullets and tear gas bombs through the jagged windows. The guard in circle No. 1 is in the act of firing through the bars at prisoners who are fighting back with everything they've got, including tommy guns and rifles. The desperadoes are in command of the center tier of the three-tier block from the northern end of the building to the seventh window, as shown by dotted line (No. 2). The guards' advance is in wartime fire-and-cover style.

How do "fortunes" start?

Men do occasionally "strike it rich" through fortunate discoveries or unexpected windfalls.

But most of our substantial fortunes were built within one lifetime, through hard work, enterprise, inventiveness, business acumen...and the *ability to save money.*

One of the best ways we know to develop this saving *habit* is to open a *Buy $1000 Plan** account. To succeed, one must make a serious start...and *keep at it.* He soon gets the *thousand-dollar habit* of thrift.

*Ask at Savings Department for leaflet describing Plan.

Wells Fargo Bank & UNION TRUST CO.
SAN FRANCISCO · 20
Market at Montgomery
Market at Grant Ave.
Established 1852
Member Federal Deposit Insurance Corporation

Here's the Story of How It Happened ---
By STANTON DELAPLANE

This is how it happened on Alcatraz:

About 2 o'clock, a pair of the toughest cons ever sent to the Big House overpowered a guard in the gun gallery catwalk and took his guns away.

Bernard P. Coy, a short, rail-thin Kentucky bank robber doing 25 years the hard way, was the ringleader.

The other was probably Joseph Paul Cretzer, a murderer who was the Nation's No. 1 bank robber. As events shaped up, Cretzer went stir crazy when he got a gun back in his fist.

Only a few years ago, Cretzer and Arnold Kyle blazed a trail of crime through the West. Cretzer was married to Kyle's sister who ran a Contra Costa County house of prostitution. An unsavory mob who went through hell in snarling defiance of law.

No one knows this morning exactly how Cretzer and Coy got into the screened, locked gun gallery overlooking the cell block.

Some reports said they pried a bar loose.

They slugged Guard Bert Burch, got his rifle and pistol and about a hundred rounds of ammunition. Then Coy threw
Continued on Page 4, Col. 3

Casualty List In the Battle Of Alcatraz

Dead and wounded in the Alcatraz revolt are:

DEAD:
Harold P. Stites, guard, shot through the back.

WOUNDED:
Fred J. Richberger, guard, wounded in calf of leg.
Harry Cochrane, guard, wounded badly in upper left arm near shoulder.
Robert Sutter, guard, slight nose wound.
Elmus Besk, guard, leg and face wounds.
Herschel R. Oldham, officer, wounds in left arm, hand and other parts of the body.
Joseph Simpson, Lieutenant, shot several times in stomach. "Condition critical."
Henry H. Weinhold, Captain, unspecified wounds; critical condition.
Continued on Page 7, Col. 8

All Hostages Believed Freed as Battle Continues After 13 Hours
By EDWARD B. McQUADE

An inferno of gunfire between guards and rioting convicts still engulfed the Federal penitentiary on Alcatraz Island early this morning after a day and night of one of the bloodiest prison uprisings in California history.

One guard was killed and at least 16 guards and an undetermined number of convicts wounded in a pitched battle that started raging at 2 p. m. yesterday.

After 13 hours of continuous fighting, the guards early today had forced the rioters back into a cell block in the western wing of the main cell house, and were pressing their attack furiously.

Here the battle was waged desperately in the dark, the only black spot on an island that otherwise was a ring of fire in the night, outlined harshly by searchlights and the blinking beacons of ceaselessly patrolling gun boats.

The tide of battle turned shortly after midnight, when the besieging guards freed eight of their comrades who had been held as hostages by the rioters. So far as was known this released all hostages.

All the hostages were seriously wounded. They had been shot and slugged by their captors, who had raged about "like mad dogs," firing point blank at their victims. Fire of the hostages escaped only by "playing dead" during their captivity.

The dead man, Guard Harold P. Stites, was killed by machine gun fire in the warders' first counter attack on the insurrectionists late yesterday afternoon.

The day and night of horror began at 2 p. m. when two of the felons' ringleaders gained entry to the arsenal of Block D of the center tier of the three-tier cell block.

These were Bernard P. Coy,
Continued on Page 7, Col.

More on Pages 7, 9, 10 and 11

Alcatraz was the Isle of Pelicans to the Spanish; now it is an island of steel and submachine guns. A history of Alcatraz and a description of its 1946 layout is on Page 9. On the same page is a picture of Harry Cochrane, guard who was wounded yesterday. Page 10 is a complete page of pictures of the uprising, a diagram of the island and an inside view of the cell block. Two Chronicle reporters, only 50 yards from the island aboard boats, give eye-witness accounts on Page 11 of the guards' first attack. Also on 11 are pictures of San Franciscans watching the battle from the Marina.

bank robber, and Joseph Paul Cretzer, murderer and bank robber.

How they got into the ar
Continued on Page 7, Col.

DEMONSTRATIONS AND ESCAPES

Demonstrations

Every now and then the inmates would act up as a group. One incident happened during the evening meal in the dining room. All of a sudden the inmates started picking up the benches and tables, and their silverware and trays, and throwing them all over the place. Before long it was a full-scale riot.

Sometimes when we had problems in that area—in a corner or something—we could go right in and take care of it. This was different, because it was obviously premeditated. Everything happened too fast to be spontaneous.

The lieutenant on duty took one look at me and another officer, and told us to pick up a couple of rifles and go man the gun gallery outside the dining room. Believe me, I was glad to be on the outside.

When the disturbance continued, we were ordered to break the glass and shove our rifles through to intimidate the prisoners. One inmate managed to creep along the side of the wall out of sight and grab one of the rifle barrels. We all had slings on the rifles and, although the officer was slammed against the side of the gallery, he was able to hang on. If the inmate had gotten that rifle inside the dining room, there would have been blood from one end of the place to the other—theirs and ours.

The biggest problem with an incident like that is that in the beginning we were never sure if it was a riot or a breakout, and there's quite a difference. A breakout is much more serious; officers are generally taken hostage, and often killed. A riot is more of a demonstration, the inmates' way of simply saying they wanted something changed, and didn't feel the administration was listening.

This particular episode lasted for over a half hour, which is quite a long time for a demonstration. We were ready at all times to trigger the teargas canisters mounted on the walls. If that had happened, the next step would have been to try to get gas masks in to the officers trapped inside. Fortunately, that didn't come about and we were able to quiet the inmates down. I believe they eventually met with some prison officials, spoke their piece, and

Front page of the *San Francisco Chronicle* Friday, May 3, 1946. *Courtesy* San Francisco Chronicle.

UNITED STATES DEPARTMENT OF JUSTICE
UNITED STATES PENITENTIARY
ALCATRAZ ISLAND, CALIFORNIA

May 16, 1950

Correctional Officer Frank J. Heaney
Alcatraz Island, California

Dear Mr. Heaney:

    This is to commend you for your extremely cooperative attitude in responding immediately to the emergency situation created by the inmates of this institution during the dining room disturbance on the evening of May 15, 1950. There is no doubt in my mind that your quick response, along with other members of the staff, prevented the disturbance from becoming a truly serious situation.

    It is thought fitting that a copy of this letter be placed with your personnel records for future reference.

Sincerely,

E. B. SWOPE
Warden

Left: View of mess hall tear-gas release switchboard in Alcatraz. Officers were prepared to use these if necessary to quell the riot in the dining room. *Courtesy National Maritime Museum, San Francisco.*

Right: Letter of commendation to Frank from Warden Swope in recognition of his role during the dining room riot in 1950.

were sent back to their cells.

Then there was a complete lockdown for one week: no work, sandwiches inside the cells, no activities, while the ring-leaders were interrogated. Some spent time in solitary, and a lot spent time in isolation in the D-Block area.

I received a commendation letter from the Warden for my part in helping to control the situation.

Early Escape Attempts

In 1936, Joe Bowers was the first man to try to escape from Alcatraz. Actually, it was more like a suicide attempt. He was apparently a simple-minded sort, and he had been put to work dumping garbage into the bay and burning papers in the incinerator on the west side of the island.

One day about noon, Bowers just got it into his head to take a hike over the fence. Of course he was easy to spot from the control tower and a guard yelled at him almost immediately to stop. When he didn't, the guard fired one shot. Bowers just kept going, so the guard decided he'd better try to wound him.

The rifles the guards had were .30-06 and extremely powerful. I know from firing them myself that they were difficult to maneuver and especially hard to balance. When the officer took a shot at Bowers, he was aiming to hit him in the legs. But the force was so great that Bowers fell over the side of the cliff and down to the rocks below. He died from his injuries in the fall.

In 1945, a guy name John Giles made another escape attempt. His prison job was as a dock worker and, as I recall, a gardener down around the shoreline area of the island. He was going on 50 and knew he didn't have enough poop in him to make the swim, so he devised another way to get out.

Once a week *The General Cox* (the supply boat) came in from Fort Mason, stopped at Alcatraz, and then went on to Angel Island, which was an army base at that time. It was carrying a cargo of uniforms, so it wasn't difficult for Giles to steal a technical sergeant's uniform and hide it in the gardener's shack.

The day he had picked to take off, Giles snuck the uniform down underneath the dock and, when the guards' backs were turned, he crawled under the dock and wriggled into the army clothing. Then he slipped in with some of the soldiers on the dock and nobody noticed a thing. Apparently they weren't quite as strict with the inmates down in that area, because he was able to get onto the boat and head for Angel Island.

But just as the boat took off, one of the guards noticed that Giles wasn't around, and it didn't take much to figure out that there was only one place he could be. So the associate warden grabbed one of our boats and took off for Angel Island too. When Giles landed, they were there ready and waiting with a set of handcuffs for him.

That earned Giles the nickname of "Sarge." I knew him when

Upper: Mug shot of Marvin Hubbard, taken in Alabama. Hubbard was killed during the 1946 seige. *Courtesy National Maritime Museum, San Francisco.*

Lower: Mug Shot of Bernard Coy, killed during the 1946 seige. *Courtesy National Maritime Museum.*

he did his time in isolation. When they finally let him out of isolation in 1949, believe it or not, he went back to being a gardener on the western side of the island. One of my duties was to shake down his potting shed, so I had a chance to talk to him quite a bit. He didn't say much, but he did like to tell the story of his escape attempt and it *was* interesting.

Having tried to escape was one of the few things that set prisoners apart from one another, and so it was quite a big deal among the cons to have tried at least once to get out. (And apparently it was in the back of their minds a lot, even if there was no realistic chance that they would ever make an attempt. A young priest who came over to work with the Catholic chaplain said that at first the prisoners ignored him, until they learned he coached a swimming team—suddenly he had become the center of attention.)

The Blast-out

The Blast-out started on Thursday, May 2, 1946. The six men who instigated the rebellion had a complaint record totaling sixteen previous escapes (from other institutions). Three of them were serving life sentences, one was in for ninety-nine years, one for thirty years, and one for twenty-five. Seven warrants had been filed against them for other offenses, and all of them had used firearms in committing their previous crimes. Why shouldn't they try to break out of Alcatraz? What did they have to lose?

When the breakout began, William Miller was the only officer on the floor of the main cellblock, and Bert Burch was the only armed officer in the entire prison. Burch was stationed in the west gun gallery which overlooked the inmate areas. He had to make periodic visits to D-Block, the isolation ward.

The majority of the inmates had just finished their noon meal and were back at their work stations. Some were in the shops; a few of the kitchen crew had been allowed into the recreation yard.

Several prisoners were assigned to a cleanup crew in the kitchen area. One was Marvin Hubbard, a man who had stolen a machine gun and several revolvers and escaped from a prison in Alabama. In the main cellhouse, orderly Bernard Coy awaited his chance. (When Coy had been sentenced to Alcatraz, he had made the statement that murder meant nothing to him and that no prison could hold him. I suppose he was out to prove it.)

It was 1:40 in the afternoon. Hubbard left the kitchen area and walked over to the cellhouse. Officer Miller opened the door and leaned over to give him the routine search. By prearranged plan, inmate Sam Shockley had started a disturbance in his isolation cell and had lured Officer Burch, the gun gallery officer, over to D-Block.

Hubbard was armed with a knife he had stolen from the kitchen, and Coy and Hubbard together jumped Miller. They beat him, tied him up, and placed him in the cell at the end of C-Block. They confiscated all of Miller's keys, with one exception: the key they needed most, the one to the recreation yard where a number of prisoners were waiting to join in the escape attempt. They missed that key when they first imprisoned Miller, and he later was able to hide it in the cell toilet.

Coy and Hubbard immediately set to unlocking the cells of several inmates they had chosen previously to help in the escape. Joe Cretzer was one of them. He had admitted to nine daylight bank robberies, and he had tried to escape from McNeil Island while he was on trial. During that attempt, he had assaulted a U.S. marshall, who had subsequently died of a heart attack; Cretzer had been convicted of causing his death.

They were joined by inmate Clarence Carnes, the Choctaw Indian and murderer, kidnapper, and escape artist, who they posted as a look-out.

With no one else in the way, Coy and Hubbard opened the doors to the utility corridor. They had one threaded pipe to use as a bar spreader, and the plan was to enter the gun gallery. I've been told that Coy had lost a lot of weight so he would be able to squeeze through tight spaces. At any rate, he was the one to squirm through the bars and make it to the door of D-Block.

On the other side of the door was Officer Bert Burch. Coy made a noise and crouched down so Burch couldn't see him through the vision panel. Just as Burch moved towards the door, he looked back over his shoulder, and that was all the opportunity Coy needed.

With one heave, he shoved open the door, threw Burch off balance, and floored him. They struggled for his weapon and somehow Coy got hold of Burch's necktie; he was able to choke him until he fell unconscious. Coy tied him up with the cord used to lower the keys down to the floorman, and took his 38-automatic revolver.

Coy then passed the revolver down to Cretzer, kept a rifle for himself, and proceeded to the D-Block area in the isolation unit. When Cretzer walked into that area, Officer Corwin, who was unarmed, made a move like he was going to try to get to the telephone. Cretzer screamed, "Lay down, you son of a bitch, or I'll kill you!" He made Officer Corwin open the ground floor steel door between the isolation area and the main prison.

Cretzer wanted to release Whitey Franklin, a fellow who had murdered an officer in 1938, but Franklin was in the isolation wing. He was serving two life sentences plus thirty years for bank robbery. He had a daring way about him that Cretzer admired, and he thought Franklin was just the man they needed to help in the escape attempt.

But solitary cells were operated by electric controls from the upper areas, and the escapees couldn't figure out how to work them. They couldn't release any of the ground floor prisoners either, because their cells were also electrically operated from the gun gallery above.

When Clarence Carnes saw they were armed, he said "Let's

Upper: Joseph Paul Cretzer, killed during the 1946 seige. *Courtesy National Maritime Museum, San Francisco.*

Lower: Mug shot of Myron E. Thompson, executed at San Quentin for his role in the 1946 blastout. *Courtesy National Maritime Museum, San Francisco.*

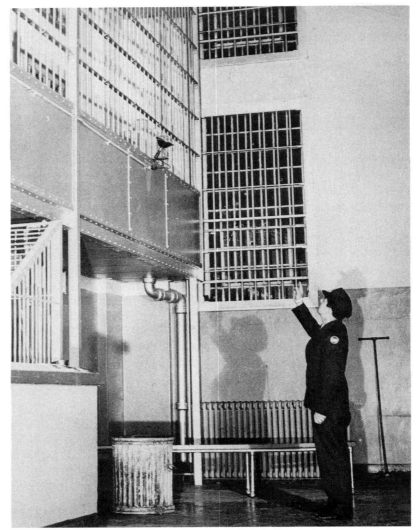

Left: Prison key, similar to the one the guards managed to hide, foiling the attempt to break out of prison during the 1946 blastout. *Courtesy National Maritime Museum, San Francisco.*

Right: Officer pointing to area where Bernard Coy entered the gun gallery using a bar spreader during the 1946 blastout. *Courtesy Golden Gate National Recreation Area.*

take over the joint!" He later told me that, instead of going from the yard to the lookout tower to the dock, their plan had been to go up one of the skylights in the cellhouse, work their way across the roof, and somehow get down into the armory. He had been told there was a tunnel leading down to the dock, which wasn't true.

They thought that by getting to the armory they could get enough weapons to take control of the entire island; then they could cut off communications with the mainland, take hostages, and get a boat. It always sounded like a crazy scheme to me, and I don't know how they ever thought they could pull it off, but that was Clarence's tale to me.

The escape group opened several more cell areas. They released another of their co-conspirators. Miran Thompson, a lifer with a long record of crime, including kidnapping and murdering a police officer. But many of the prisoners stayed by their doors. Sizing up the situation, they were leary of what was going on. They started milling in and out and soon they were all quite agitated. That's when Sam Shockley was released and joined the group. He had been serving a life sentence for bank robbery, kidnapping, and several escapes, and he had been involved with Cretzer before.

So now there were six inmates involved at the west end of the cellhouse on the ground floor level. They had a good view of anyone who tried to enter through the gate, and they could see the lock on the corridor in front of them without exposing any of their own positions.

There were firearms inside the building, and Coy had his rifle, Cretzer had the automatic, and Hubbard had a carving knife. Carnes had grabbed a club and a pair of calipers which he held as a dagger, and Shockley was carrying a heavy wrench.

None of them could open the main door leading to the yard—an important area because the plan at this point was to pick off the tower guard, get his weapons, and climb over the wall and take control of the island.

Finally, they went back in and started beating and kicking Officer Miller in an attempt to get the right key. Cretzer was really losing it by now, and he screamed, "You know I can't find the goddamn key! We're all fouled up and Frisco's as far away as ever!"

Just then the dining room steward, Bristow, who had been in the administration office for a conference, walked into the cellhouse unaware of what was happening. He was on his way to his station in the kitchen when he saw Hubbard and Carnes. Carnes put a choke hold on him, shoved the calipers up to his throat, and threw him in a cell with Miller and Corwin.

Then another correctional officer, Officer Lageson, who had just finished his lunch and was proceeding down Broadway—the main area—was jumped by Coy and Cretzer and thrown in the same cell. About ten minutes later, Officer Burdette, who was working in the back of the kitchen, saw Coy going past the door leading to the dining room. He thought Coy was involved in a fight with another prisoner and rushed out right into Hubbard.

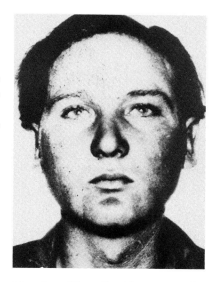

Mug shot of Sam Shockley, executed at San Quentin with Thompson for his role in the 1946 blastout. *Courtesy National Maritime Museum, San Francisco.*

Pretty soon, he was in the same cell with all the others.

It was just about that time that Officer Ed Stucker (I knew him quite well and still see him at the Annual Alcatraz Alumni Association Meeting) went on duty in the basement bath house and clothing room. He sent several prisoners to the top of the stairs to be checked back into the cellhouse. When his prisoners came back saying there was no guard at the door, Stucker didn't know what was going on. He went to the top of the stairs himself to look for Miller; when he couldn't see anything, he knew something was amiss and he telephoned the armory. He told Captain Weinhold he thought perhaps there was a fight in the kitchen area.

Weinhold, Lieutenant Simpson, and Officers Sundstrom and Baker (whom I knew from Berkeley as our mailman) all took off for the cellhouse. Captain Weinhold, who was a burly ex-Marine, headed straight for the kitchen where he thought there was trouble to be settled. There was trouble all right: when he got to the west end of the cellhouse, he was jumped by Coy, Carnes, *and* Hubbard.

The prisoners were a bit undecided as to whether to put him in the same cell with other guards or to lock him in another part of the prison. Weinhold was *really* not well liked.

They finally decided to stick him in Carnes' cell and made him remove all his clothes and trade with Coy. Then all four of them moved him to the hostage cell. Shockley was going a little nuts now, and he tried to punch the captain in the face; Weinhold ducked and Shockley hit him in the back.

Lieutenant Simpson, and Baker and Sundstrom were next, and they soon met the same fate as Captain Weinhold. By this time, it was so crowded that they had to put these three in Cell 402. The armed prisoners now had nine officers as hostages: Weinhold, Miller, Corwin, Burdette, Bristow, and Lageson in Cell 403. And Simpson, Baker, and Sundstrom in Cell 402.

It was about 2:30 p.m., and Officer Fish was trying to call the west gun gallery from the armory. When he got no response, he

[As reported by the press] *Ernest Lageson lay among the dying and wounded colleagues as last May's bloody revolt filled Alcatraz's main cell block with exploding shells. He reached up—so he told a Federal Court jury—and scribbled the names of ringleaders on the cell wall. This photo became Government Exhibit No. 25 in the trial of Miran Edgar Thompson, Clarence Carnes, and Sam Shockley for the mutiny slaying of Guard William A. Miller. And Lageson thus put the finger on that trio as conspirators. The ringed names are those of convicts Marvin Hubbard, Bernard Coy and "Dutch Joe" Cretzer, all slain. Courtesy* San Francisco Chronicle.

called Associate Warden Miller, affectionately known as "Meathead" by the prisoners, who grabbed a gas billy.

Miller headed for the cellhouse, spotted Coy, and saw that he was well armed, so he turned to escape before Coy could reload and shoot him. In his haste he struck the gas billy against a concrete overhang and it exploded into his face. Miller came flying out of there all burned, with his face blackened and his eyes smarting.

Now the guards knew they were in trouble. All off-duty officers were called back, and an official state-of-emergency was declared. Warden Johnston was notified and the alarm was sounded.

The first rescue attempts started at about 10:00 p.m., when fourteen armed officers stormed the front gates and went down between C- and D-Blocks. They were immediately hit with a round of gunfire, had to back-track, but finally worked their way into Cells 402 and 403.

Burdette, Bristow, and Sundstrom were not hurt. Lageson had been shot in the cheek, but it was a superficial wound. The other officers were not so lucky; Baker had two serious wounds on his left leg, and the remaining four were really in bad shape.

The rescue squad laid them out on stretchers outside the office area and public health doctors were brought in to attend to them. Miller had a deep wound in his right arm. Captain Weinhold had been shot in the arm and chest. Lieutenant Simpson had been shot twice also, once in the abdomen and once in the chest. But Corwin was the worst; his face was unrecognizable. Only by process of elimination could they identify him. He had been shot point-blank in the head. The 45-caliber bullet entered near the left eye and came out about an inch below his right ear.

The uninjured hostages quickly told the story of what had happened to them. The escapees had become more and more agitated when they couldn't find the right keys to the yard area, and had started threatening the captive officers. Cretzer had stood, with his pistol in his hands, in front of Cell 403. Captain Weinhold had tried to talk him into surrendering his weapon and giving up the escape attempt.

Weinhold said, "You can't get away with it, Cretzer. You can't even get to the yard. Even if you do get out there, someone's going to get hurt. It's best to give up now. The sirens are going to go off any minute."

Cretzer replied, "You mean somebody's gonna get killed? Well, you're gonna be the first son of a bitch to die."

"I can only die once," said Weinhold. At that exact instant, the sirens did go off. Cretzer panicked. He put the pistol between the bars and pulled the trigger. Weinhold fell to the floor but Cretzer kept shooting. Then he turned the gun on Miller and Corwin and got them too. It was just like shooting fish in a barrel.

Then he went to the next cell and shot Lieutenant Simpson, hit Baker, and fired at Sundstrom who fell to the floor without being hit. Now Shockley and Thompson were frantic, scared, and excited all at the same time. They kept shouting, "Kill all the sons of bitches! Kill the bastards! Kill 'em! Don't leave any witnesses!"

Under their prodding, and with Bernard Coy shouting as well, Cretzer went back to Cell 402 and shot Simpson again in the back and Baker in the legs. Sundstrom wasn't hurt at all, but Cretzer thought he was dead because he wasn't moving.

When the prisoners who had been in D-Block heard the sirens, most of them went back to their cells and waited. But Coy kept on. He was trying to pick off the tower officers and he shot anything that moved on the outside.

Shockley was half nuts anyway and, more than that, he hated officers and wanted a little piece of them for himself; so he kept telling Cretzer to keep killing.

Thompson was a little more intelligent, and when he saw that they weren't going to succeed, he slipped back to his cell and started trying to think up an alibi. Clarence Carnes did the same thing. Finally, even Shockley crept back.

So now it was down to just three: Coy, Cretzer, and Hubbard. They were still trapped, but they had their weapons and plenty of ammunition. By this time, the guards outside had surmised that the prisoners had taken over C-Block, but they weren't exactly sure which portion, and they also thought there was a possibility that there was an armed prisoner in D-Block as well.

A small tunnel connected these two cell blocks, and the guards thought there might be more armed prisoners there. The associate warden and a warrant officer who came over from the Treasure Island Marine Station made the decision that the only way to get the escapees out of there was by dropping gas grenades.

First, they tried to make contact with them, but to no avail. So, they started cutting holes in the roof with an electric drill. They dropped the grenades down through the ventilation shafts and into the utility quarters. Still there was no response.

They were sure the inmates were in the tunnel now, and kept dropping bomb after bomb. They shot more grenades down the west side of the island and, before long, the grass caught on fire and the entire building was engulfed in smoke. From San Francisco, it looked as though all of Alcatraz was on fire.

By now it was well into the night and reinforcements were being brought in on the Alcatraz launch. A detail of men from San Quentin was sent over, a hospital in San Francisco and the public health department sent aides to attend to the wounded, and the Bureau of Prisons sent officers all the way from Inglewood, McNeil Island, and Leavenworth.

The firing of grenades into D-Block continued until Robert Stroud, the "Birdman," pleaded with Lt. Bergen that there were no armed prisoners down there, and that the area was being destroyed. They must have believed him, because they shifted the focus of their firing to C-Block.

It wasn't until Saturday, May 4, at about 7:00 a.m., that they were able to shoot the three hold-outs, and the guards were fully back in control. It had taken forty-eight hours to subdue the uprising. In the final count, two officers had been killed, three prisoners were dead (Cretzer, Coy, and Hubbard), and one prisoner and fourteen officers had been wounded.

Utility corridor on C-Block where the slain bodies of Coy, Cretzer and Hubbard were found. *Courtesy Golden Gate National Recreation Area.*

Outside the main cell block during the 1946 blastout, showing guards on the hill to the left, and smoke from exploding rifle grenades which had been shot through the windows. *Courtesy National Maritime Museum, San Francisco.*

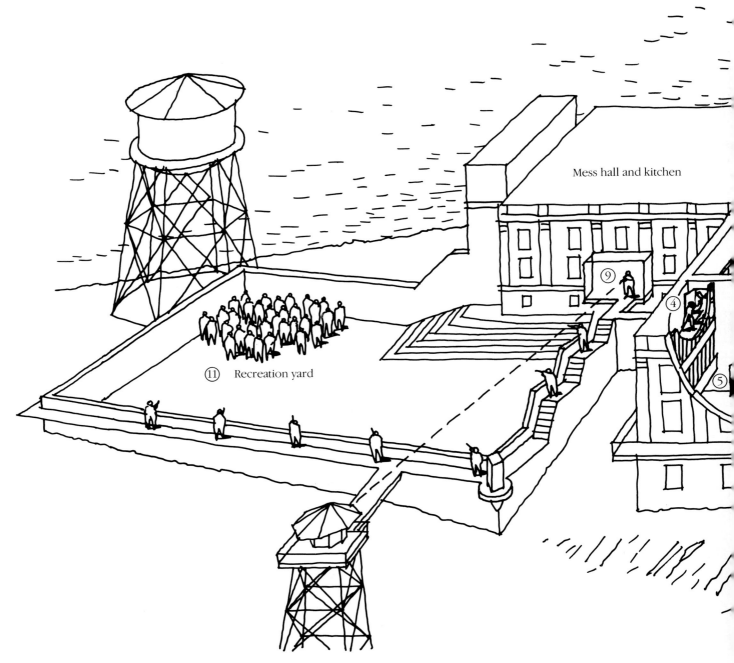

Sequence of events:
1. Coy and Hubbard slug and capture Cell House Officer Miller and take his keys.
2. Hubbard releases Cretzer, Carnes and Thompson.
3. Coy monkey-climbs cage protecting armed officer while he is in "D" block and gains access to gun-gallery by spreading bars.
4. Coy slugs armed officer Burch as he passes from "D" block to main cellhouse; captures his arms and throws a pistol down to Cretzer.
5. With rifle Coy forces "D" block officer to open door between "D" block and main cell block.
6. Cretzer rushes in with pistol and liberates 12 of worst prisoners segregated in "D" block; but is unable to release those in electrically controlled cells.
7. Reserve officers on duty in administration building, having been advised that officer Miller did not answer his call, enter main cell block to investigate.

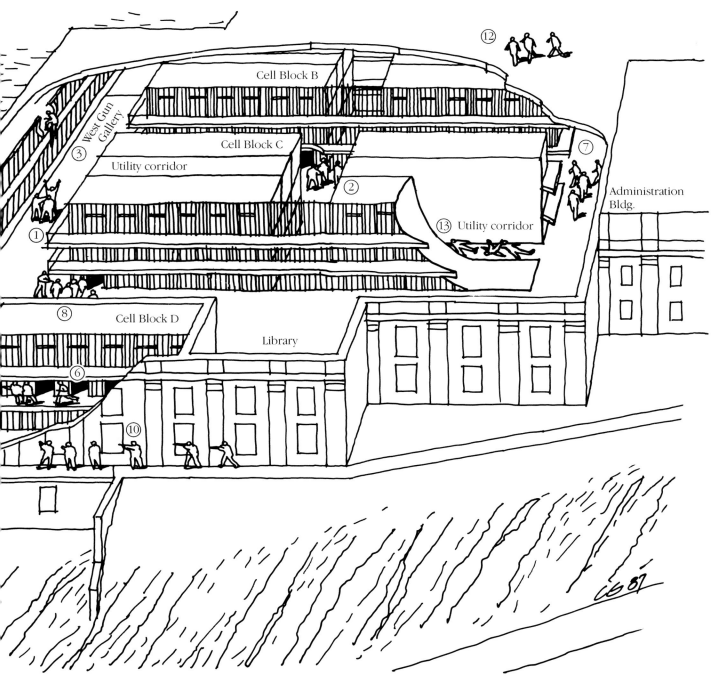

8. They are captured and locked in cell, where they were later shot by Cretzer.

9. Coy then attempts to shoot Tower officer.

10. Officers run to rear entrance and this, plus officer Miller's hiding of outside door keys, blocks escape from main cellhouse. Later, officers from this point attempt to gas "D" block through window.

11. Other prisoners not participating in revolt are herded into recreation yard, where they are guarded by Marines until prisoners in cellhouse are subdued.

12. Officers break through roof and drop grenades and bombs, finally dislodging Coy, Cretzer and Hubbard from pipe tunnel where they were driven by officers after gun battle.

13. Found dead in utilities corridor.

Courtesy National Maritime Museum, San Francisco.

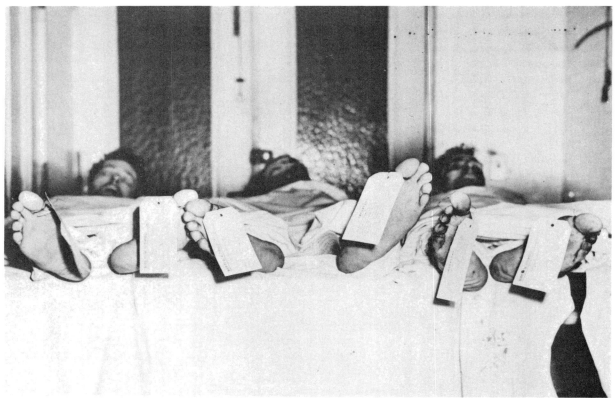

Opposite, top: (left to right) Thompson, Carnes and Shockley being led to the courtroom after 1946 blastout. *Courtesy Golden Gate National Recreation Area*

Opposite, bottom: Photo taken at San Francisco morgue of Coy, Cretzer, Hubbard, all killed during the 1946 blastout. *Courtesy Golden Gate National Recreation Area*

Above: Officer peering through peephole into the cellhouse. These were used for observation from the outside when there were emergencies inside. *Courtesy Golden Gate National Recreation Area*

WANTED BY THE FBI
ESCAPED FEDERAL PRISONER – BANK ROBBER

"Escape from Alcatraz"

In 1962 four men attempted an escape—the only one that may possibly have been successful. It later became a movie starring Clint Eastwood, called "Escape from Alcatraz." Four prisoners were involved. Clint Eastwood played the part of inmate Frank Morris. The others were the Anglin brothers, Clarence and John, and an inmate named West.

They planned to cut holes in the rear of their cells, cutting out metal grates which backed up to a utility corridor. Although there is some question about the tools used, apparently they ranged from a sharpened spoon to more sophisticated equipment smuggled from the shop. They had plaster of paris and art supplies to cover and disguise the holes they were digging. They also used plaster of paris to make dummies to leave behind in their beds.

Apparently it took weeks to complete the escape holes, but no one suspected a thing. After lights out on the evening of June 11, 1962 the four prisoners put the dummies in their beds and squeezed through the holes in the back of their cells—all but West; his hole wasn't big enough and he never got out.

The three others crawled up a ventilation duct which took them up to the top of the building. From there they were able to scale down the outside and reach the shore line. They had old raincoats fashioned into crude rafts which they had planned to blow up and use for flotation. (These and other details were learned from West.) The plan was to go to Angel Island, steal a boat there, get over to Marin county, and head north. The escape was not discovered until the morning of the 12th.

The three men left the Island and were never heard from again. As I said earlier, theoretically they may have made it, and the inmate population generally believed that they did. (When the piped-in evening radio show was suddenly cut off the evening after the break-out, the inmates knew that a news flash on the escape was being censored out, and the whole prison erupted in a sudden cheer.)

But the water was extremely cold and the tides particularly swift on that evening, running at 8 knots out the Golden Gate. The men had been in prison all of their adult lives, and were hardly in condition for long freezing swims. I agree with the general belief of the prison authorities that they all drowned.

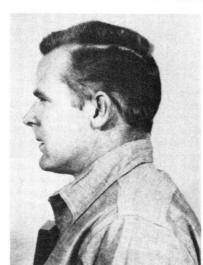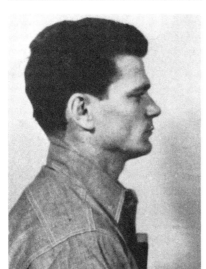

Top to bottom: Mugshots of Clarence Anglin, John Anglin, and Frank Morris—the ringleaders of the 1962 "Escape from Alcatraz." *Courtesy Golden Gate National Recreation Area*

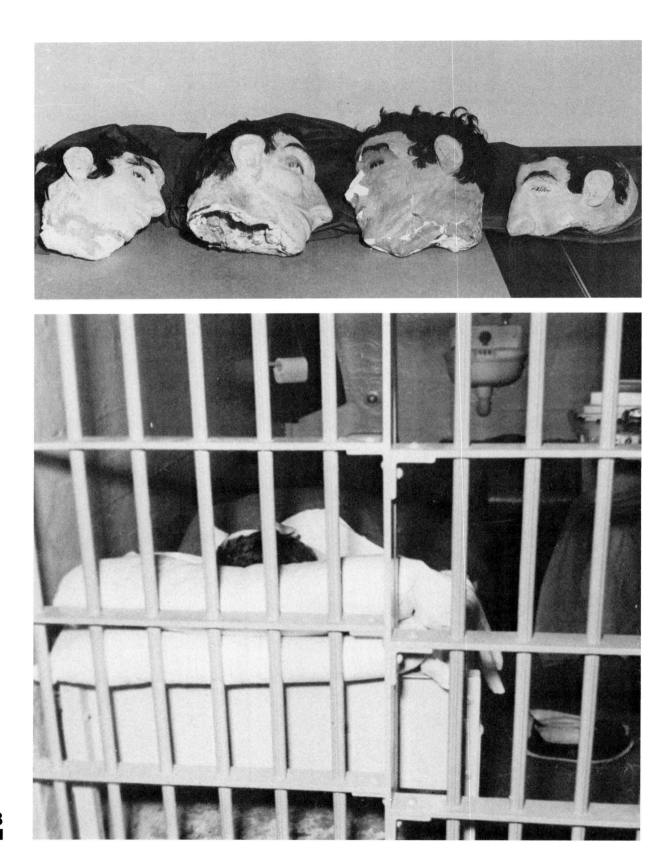

Opposite, top: Paper-mache heads used in 1962 escape. *Photo by SA F.G. Lyman, courtesy Golden Gate National Recreation Area*

Opposite bottom: Guard's view of dummy head. The human hair, smuggled from the barbershop, made the head look very real. *Courtesy Golden Gate National Recreation Area*

Below: Photograph of the tools and equipment fashioned from readily available objects by the inmates. The ones that are identifiable are as follows: lower center, sharpened spoon handles which were used in penetrating cell walls; center, the object which looks like a radio speaker is a motor removed from a vacuum cleaner and utilized as a drill; the round object immediately above the drill is a housing which was apparently fitted over the vacuum cleaner motor to quiet its noise; upper right, pieces of electrical cord; middle left, these bolts with nuts, shafts and sleeves may have been used to apply pressure in spreading bars; extreme upper left, this is a homemade flashlight using two penlight batteries, illuminated by making contact with the exposed portion of the bulb and the small piece of metal immediately above and to the right of the bulb. The other items apparently are scraping, digging, cutting and gouging tools. All of these objects had been discarded in a five-gallon paint bucket filled with liquid paint cement and allowed to harden, apparently to avoid detection. *Photo by SA F.G. Lyman, courtesy Golden Gate National Recreation Area*

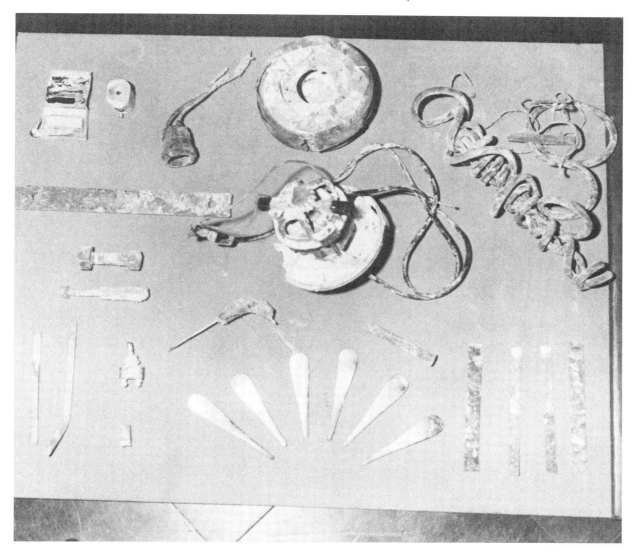

Top: Frank Morris' cell with his accordion case hiding the escape hole from view. The bellows of the accordion were used to blow up the life rafts for the escape. *Courtesy Golden Gate National Recreation Area*

Middle: Guard looking at escape hole in the rear of cell. *Courtesy Golden Gate National Recreation Area*

Bottom: The guard in the utility corridor points out the hole and dummy cover (in his hand) which masked the work. The paint on the cover was blended to match exactly that of the area around the hole. *Courtesy Golden Gate National Recreation Area*

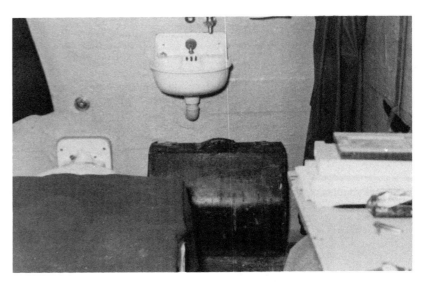
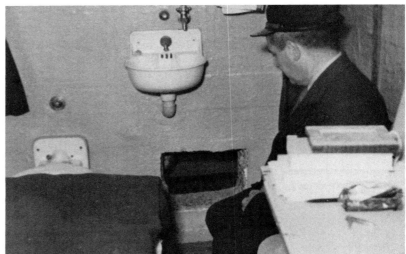

Guard looks at vent atop cell block B from which the prisoners escaped after leaving the utility corridor.
Courtesy Golden Gate National Recreation Area

The Last Escape

The last escape was attempted later in 1962, about a year before they closed the penitentiary. Two prisoners were involved, John Paul Scott and Darl Dee Parker. They were able to get out of a kitchen window, and made their way down to the shore line on the San Francisco side. They blew up some surgical gloves that they had stolen from the prison hospital, and they used these for buoyancy as they took off into the bay.

Darl Parker did not get very far. He apparently became afraid that he was going to die in the water, and only got as far as Little Alcatraz, a rock outcropping right off the island.

Scott kept on going. Their intention had been to go to Aquatic Park, right across in San Francisco, where they figured no one would notice them because there are cold water swimmers frequently in the area. But with the tide running very swiftly out towards the Golden Gate, instead of going to Aquatic Park, which was about a mile and a quarter, Scott went three miles to Fort Point, just on the San Francisco side of the Golden Gate Bridge.

By the time he got there, he was half dead from hypothermia. But in his mind he thought he had it made—he was on the beach alive. But while he was laying there two kids spotted him and felt sorry for him. They called the police.

AFTERWORD

The Death Penalty

A lot has been said for and against the death penalty, and I have my own opinions on the subject. I remember way back in 1949, about a year after I started on Alcatraz, I had a conversation with Clinton P. Duffy, the well-known Warden of San Quentin.

He was adamantly against the death penalty, and at first that puzzled me. He said the reason he felt that way was because he knew a rich man would never be sent to the chair; if you had enough money to hire a good lawyer, you might get a life sentence, but you'd never be executed.

I agreed with him for a long time—until I heard about Federal correction officers being murdered and nothing being done to their killers because they were already multiple-life inmates. That changed my mind.

Severity of Sentencing

I've done a lot of thinking about long-term sentences, and I've said a million times that they were the primary reason for the despondency and depression among the inmate population. Now I'm not saying it's wrong to have sentences equivalent to the crime, but I know this feeling of hopelessness is why most of the convicts constantly had escape on their minds. What else was there?

In addition to the punishment for Federal crimes, half the inmates on Alcatraz had some kind of detainer on them. That meant there was a hold by a state that wanted them for further imprisonment when their time was up on Alcatraz.

Was Alcatraz Necessary?

Many people ask me why we had to have prisons like Alcatraz at all. They wonder whether it didn't represent a failed system—

The last group of Alcatraz prison convicts walking down the boat ramp in 1963. *Courtesy National Maritime Museum, San Francisco*

Inmate cell in later years, reflecting a more lenient policy toward personal belongings and decorating of cells

one that had to rely on an isolated island to secure its prisoners. Well I believe that our Federal prison system is one of the best in the United States, if not the world. And there was ample justification for "the Rock."

There are different types of prisoners and different prison needs. I've visited many prisons, and the one example that comes to mind, as a contrast to Alcatraz, is Pleasanton—which is almost like a college campus—for minimum security prisoners. The inmates there are vastly different and among the easiest to control, although even there they do have different grades of security.

But Alcatraz was a product of the '30s when gangsterism was rampant, and men like Dillinger, Baby Face Nelson, and Pretty Boy Floyd were breaking out of prisons right and left. That's why we needed a place like Alcatraz. The public demanded a prison system capable of holding such men, even though at the same time they were critical of the inevitable tales of harsh treatment.

We got a lot of criticism—still do—but you've got to remember the punishment was always by degree. If an inmate kept fouling up in the system, the system got tougher. And that's the way it should be.

We were criticized most often for shooting prisoners if they tried to escape, but we had to let the others know the consequences. They weren't just risking *their* lives. They were risking *our* lives too.

You have to remember that Alcatraz received the most maladjusted inmates in the entire system. Their hatreds, prejudices, and idiosyncrasies were definitely more manifest than in the average prisoner elsewhere. You can't blame Alcatraz for the behavior of these men. They brought special problems with them. Many undoubtedly were victims of years of abuse—many going back to childhood—and of poverty, ignorance, and hopelessness.

The Closing of Alcatraz

One of the primary reasons Alcatraz was shut down was because of the cost of maintaining it. Water was expensive, the buildings were deteriorating, the foundation of the main cellhouse would soon have had to be completely torn down and rebuilt.

This was the time when Attorney General Robert Kennedy, along with many penologists, was deciding that perhaps rehabilitation was a better method than punishment in a severe environment like Alcatraz. The experiment of Alcatraz—with its severe hardships and deprivation—had become very controversial, almost an embarrassment to the "modern society" of the time.

So when Alcatraz first closed, in 1963, they tried to distribute its remaining inmates throughout the prison system—to spread the problems out. But the theory didn't work. Apparently these hard-core prisoners tended to infect their new environments.

Eventually thinking changed again. It was determined that

there does exist a very small percent of the prison population (only about 1%) that in fact must be relegated to a place like Alcatraz.

So, after about ten years of trying to be run as a normal prison, Marion Penitentiary (in Marion, Illinois) was reorganized, using Alcatraz as a model. In fact, it was made even more secure, and eventually even the prison industries were shut down because of inmate violence.

No Easy Answer

In June of 1985 these questions were addressed in testimony concerning Marion Penitentiary, before the Subcommittee on Courts, Civil Liberties, and the Administration of Justice, of the U.S. House of Representatives.

The basic issue was how to manage the country's most violent and escape-prone prisoners—whether to concentrate extreme problem prisoners into one super-security institution, or to disperse them throughout the system. Alcatraz (and now Marion) was, of course, the classic example of the former.

As far as I was concerned, those hearings finally brought back reality. Over a period of fifty years, the speakers stated, public concern had shifted from what those inmates had done to society, fellow inmates, and prison employees...to what the system of prisons had done to the inmates! These prisoners—vicious, violent people—had been romanticized in newspapers, films, and on television, to the point where they were actually arousing sympathy for *their* plight.

I believe there is a definite need for a place like Alcatraz. It should be used only as a last resort, but always for that small group of violent and extreme offenders who violate—and will continue to harm their fellow human beings...even while they're behind bars.

In many ways, life inside a prison is the same as life on the outside. There will always be that small group who, for whatever the reason, will continue to break the rules and take advantage of others.

It is my belief—and I was there—that our only solution, our only *protection*, is truly to isolate them.

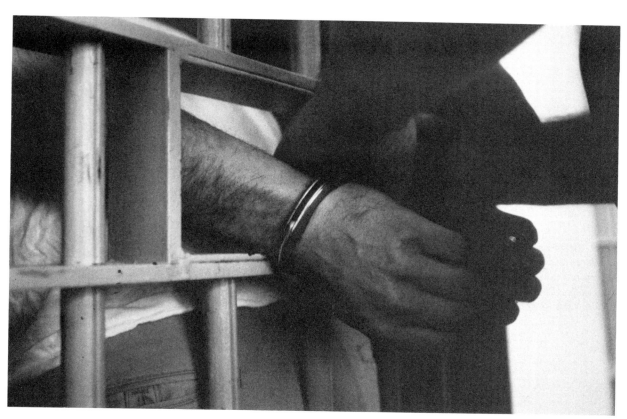

The Federal penitentiary at Marion, Illinois is today's Alcatraz. In areas of tightened security inmates are handcuffed before they leave their cells. *Photo by Kevin Manning, courtesy the* St. Louis Post-Dispatch

Questions frequently asked about "Inside the Walls of Alcatraz"

MURDER IN THE FIRST™

The Warner Bros. Feature Film Staring Kevin Bacon, Christian Slater and Gary Oldman

Fact or Fiction?

According to the Movie

1) Henri Young was sent to Alcatraz as an impoverished teenager during the Depression after stealing $5 from a Post Office to buy food for his younger sister.

2) Henri Young spent 3 years in a dungeon after his escape attempt from Alcatraz in 1939.

3) Young murdered a fellow inmate a few hours after release from isolation.

4) Young was found dead in his cell following his return to Alcatraz after winning his case against the prison system.

4a) Young died in prison.

5) The warden of Alcatraz was incompetent and uninvolved.

6) There were not enough tough cases like Al Capone or "Machine Gun" Kelly, therefore the prison authorities had to fill up Alcatraz with petty criminals.

8) Alcatraz was a prison filled with rats and squalor.

9) The Young case had a direct bearing on Alcatraz closing.

What Really Happened

1) Henri Young was a bank robber and murderer who had been incarcerated in State prison in Washington & Montana before entering Federal prison at 23 as an incorrigible.

2) Henri Young spent a few months in one or two regular cellhouses where all discipline cases were held and then returned to the general population.

3) Young murdered a fellow inmate 1 year after his return to the general population.

4) Young stayed in Alcatraz until 1948 before being transferred to the Federal prison in Missouri. He was then turned over to the Washington State Penitentiary at Walla Walla to begin a life sentence for a murder he committed in 1933.

4a) Young was paroled by Washington State authorities in 1972.

5) Warden James Johnston was regarded by scholars of American Corrections as one of the most enlightened and reform-minded prison administrators of his generation.

6) The inmate population was purposely kept low. Alcatraz's primary function was to house inmates who were so disruptive they could not be held in other Federal prisons.

8) Alcatraz was well maintained with inmate work crews on detail every day. There were regular inspections from headquarters and from a Public Health Service physician in charge of Sanitation.

9) Alcatraz was closed due to outmoded design and prohibitively high operating costs by Attorney General Robert F. Kennedy in 1963 following a series of spectacular escape attempts.